The Readers' Advisory Guide to Street Literature

ALA READERS' ADVISORY SERIES

The Readers' Advisory Guide to Street Literature,
Second Edition

The Readers' Advisory Guide to Genre Blends for
Children and Young Adults

The Readers' Advisory Guide to Horror,
Third Edition

The Readers' Advisory Guide to Genre Fiction,
Third Edition

The Readers' Advisory Guide to Teen Literature

The Readers' Advisory Guide to Graphic Novels,
Second Edition

The Readers' Advisory Guide to Genre Blends

The Readers' Advisory Guide to Historical Fiction

The Readers' Advisory Guide to Mystery,
Second Edition

The Readers' Advisory Handbook

Serving Boys through Readers' Advisory

Research-Based Readers' Advisory

Serving Teens through Readers' Advisory

The Readers' Advisory Guide to Nonfiction

The Readers' Advisory Guide to Street Literature

SECOND EDITION

VANESSA IRVIN
Foreword by Kafi D. Kumasi

ALA READERS' ADVISORY SERIES

ALA EDITIONS | 2024

VANESSA IRVIN is an associate professor of library science within the College of Education at East Carolina University, Greenville, North Carolina. With a frontline librarian career spanning over four decades, Irvin teaches reference and information services, public libraries, and reading response in library settings. Irvin's research integrates cultural heritage methodologies with librarians' work practices for professional learning and development. Irvin has a Doctorate of Education from the University of Pennsylvania.

© 2024 by Vanessa Irvin

Extensive effort has gone into ensuring the reliability of the information in this book; however, the publisher makes no warranty, express or implied, with respect to the material contained herein.

ISBN: 979-8-89255-569-2 (paper)

Library of Congress Cataloging-in-Publication Data
Names: Irvin, Vanessa, author; foreword by Kafi D. Kumasi.
Title: The readers' advisory guide to street literature / Vanessa Irvin.
Description: Second edition. | Chicago : ALA Editions, 2024. | Series: ALA readers' advisory series | Includes bibliographical references and index. | Summary: "This book explores street literature from the context of readers' advisory, including how to get up to speed quickly in street lit, using a practical guide to the genre, and emphasizing the appreciation of these titles in library communities"— Provided by publisher.
Identifiers: LCCN 2024002622 | ISBN 9798892555692 (paperback)
Subjects: LCSH: Urban fiction, American—Bibliography. | Urban fiction, American— History and criticism. | Street life—Fiction—Bibliography. | Young adult fiction, American—Bibliography. | Readers' advisory services—United States. | Fiction in libraries.
Classification: LCC Z1231.U73 M67 2024 PS374.U73 | DDC 016.813/609358209732—dc23
LC record available at https://lccn.loc.gov/2024002622

Cover design by Alejandra Diaz; imagery © Adobe Stock.
Text design and composition by Alejandra Diaz in the Source Serif Pro and Source Sans typefaces.

♾ This paper meets the requirements of ANSI/NISO Z39.48-1992 (Permanence of Paper).

Printed in the United States of America
28 27 26 25 24   5 4 3 2 1

ALA Editions purchases fund advocacy, awareness, and accreditation programs for library professionals worldwide.

CONTENTS

Series Introduction, by Joyce Saricks and Neal Wyatt   *vii*
Foreword, by Kafi D. Kumasi   *ix*
Introduction: The Canonical Agency of Street Lit   *xiii*

1   **History of Street Literature in American Literacy Culture**   1

2   **Characteristics of Street Lit**   11

3   **Understanding, Classifying, and Defining Street Lit**   27

4   **Readers' Advisory Approaches to Street Lit**   39

5   **Collection Management Considerations for Street Lit**   63

6   **Library Programming for Street Lit**   81

7   **Reading Street Lit as a Literacy Practice**   93

Epilogue: Street Lit's Enduring Legacy   *105*
Appendix: Street/Urban Literature—A Foundational Collection   *109*
References   *119*
Index   *129*

SERIES INTRODUCTION

JOYCE SARICKS AND NEAL WYATT, SERIES EDITORS

In a library world in which finding answers to readers' advisory (RA) questions is often considered among our most daunting service challenges, library staff need guides that are supportive, accessible, and immediately useful. The titles in this series are designed to be just that. They help advisors become familiar with fiction genres and nonfiction subjects, especially those they don't personally read. They provide ready-made lists of "need to know" elements such as key authors and read-alikes, as well as tips on how to keep up with trends and important new authors and titles.

Written by librarians with years of RA experience who are also enthusiasts of the genre or subject, the titles in this series of practical guides emphasize an appreciation of the topic, focusing on the elements and features fans enjoy, so advisors unfamiliar with the topics can readily appreciate why they are so popular.

Because this series values the fundamental concepts of RA work and its potential to serve readers, viewers, and listeners in whatever future-space libraries inhabit, the focus of each book is on appeal and how appeal crosses genre, subject, and format, especially to include audio and video as well as graphic novels. Thus, each guide emphasizes the importance of whole collection readers' advisory and explores ways to make suggestions that include novels, nonfiction, and multimedia, as well as how to incorporate whole collection elements into displays and booklists.

Each guide includes sections designed to help librarians in their RA duties, be those daily work or occasional interactions. Topics covered in each volume include

- The appeal of the genre or subject and information on subgenres and types so that librarians might understand the breadth and scope of the topic and how it relates to other genres and subjects. A brief history is also included to give advisors context and highlight beloved classic titles.

vii

Series Introduction

- Descriptions of key authors and titles with explanations of why they're important: why advisors should be familiar with them and why they should be kept in our collections. Lists of read-alikes accompany these core author and title lists, allowing advisors to move from identifying a key author to helping patrons find new authors to enjoy.
- Information on how to conduct the RA conversation so that advisors can learn the tools and skills needed to develop deeper connections between their collections and their communities of readers, listeners, and viewers.
- A crash course in the genre or subject is designed to get staff up to speed. Turn to this section to get a quick overview of the genre or subject as well as a list of key authors and read-alikes.
- Resources and techniques for keeping up to date and understanding new developments in the genre or subject are also provided. This section will not only aid staff already familiar with the genre or subject, but will also help those not familiar learn how to become so.
- Tips for marketing collections and lists of resources and awards round out the tools staff need to be successful working with their community.

As readers who just happen to be readers' advisors, we hope that the guides in this series lead to larger to-be-read, -watched, and -listened-to piles. Our goal is that the series helps those new to RA feel supported and less at sea, and introduces new ideas or new ways of looking at foundational concepts to advisors who have been at this a while. Most of all, we hope that this series helps advisors feel excited and eager to help patrons find their next great title. So dig in, explore, learn, and enjoy the almost alchemical process of connecting title and reader.

FOREWORD

KAFI D. KUMASI

It's been fifty years since the birth of hip-hop, which seems like both a lifetime and a mere drop in the bucket on humanity's grand time line. Similarly, the meaning of the term "street literature" has evolved in a way that illuminates the essence of hip-hop. Hip-hop is an idea that is grounded in both the now (aka "The New School") and the past (aka "The Old School"). In this second edition of *The Readers' Advisory Guide to Street Literature*, Dr. Vanessa Irvin helps readers discern the Old School origins of street literature from its New School pinnacle, which happens to coincide with the zenith of hip-hop in the late 1970s and early 1980s. Irvin's treatment of the subject matter is fortified by personal anecdotes from her experiences as a public librarian in inner-city Philadelphia, sample book titles, and scholarly references that reflect her library and information science research background.

Irvin's depiction of street literature maps nicely onto the hip-hop vernacular terms of "Old School" and "New School." In a recent podcast episode of *The Grio Daily* on the topic "What Is the Blackest Music?," Michael Harriot breaks down the difference between Old School music and music that is merely enjoyed by elderly people. For example, Harriot cites music by the band Earth, Wind and Fire as an example of Old School music because their music is still enjoyed by young people today despite it being produced four and five decades ago. By contrast, Harriot considers country music as simply "old music" because it is typically consumed by older people, especially in the context of Black American music listeners.

In this book, Irvin describes the kind of street literature that could be placed into an Old School category as those gritty tales of Black Americans living in inner cities during the 1960s and '70s. These Old School works include titles such as Claude Brown's *Manchild in the Promised Land* (1965) and Donald Goines's *Black Girl Lost* (1973). Evidence that these titles are Old School and not simply "old" is that librarians still recommend these titles to readers some fifty years after their publication. These titles are enjoyed today in the same spirit as when someone plays a "throwback" record by a pioneering hip-hop group like Grandmaster Flash and the Furious Five, who formed in the South Bronx of New York City in 1978. By contrast, Irvin describes the conservative origins of the term "street literature," which refers to written works that were pedaled in the streets of Europe during the 1700s. According to this definition, one might classify the Declaration of Independence as a form of street literature, which is ironic given that street literature has evolved into capturing everyday neighborhood dramas rather than austere political documents now attributed to the white establishment in the US.

While it is true, as Irvin writes, that some authors sold their works on the street because publishers rejected them for their gritty content, it is also true that some of the most successful authors in this genre embraced one of hip-hop's core principles—street entrepreneurialism. These authors took more of a self-determined social justice route to getting their work published and distributed. Vickie M. Stringer is an excellent example of a Black author who turned rejection by mainstream (white) publishing companies into starting her own company, Triple Crown Publications, and published *Let That Be the Reason* in 2001. When asked what made Triple Crown so successful, Stringer stated, "We know our market. What we write is not urban fiction. It's not street fiction. It's hip hop. We have addressed an audience that has said to the world, 'This is the music we want to listen to, this is the way we want to dress': Now they're saying: 'This is what they want to read'" (Stringer quoted in Murray, 2004).

Stringer linked hip-hop, street literature, and the social justice ideology that undergirds them both. She and other authors and publishers of color (e.g., Teri Woods's Meow Meow Productions and Carl Weber's Urban Books) pushed back against the all-white world of book publishing by taking control of their stories and the entire publication process, including marketing and distribution. This ethos of street entrepreneurialism crossed over into a few other hip-hop cultural realms, including music and fashion. For example, rapper Master P famously rejected a million-dollar record deal from Interscope Records executive Jimmy Iovine. He went on to sell millions of records under his own label, No Limit Records, while also building a diverse portfolio of wealth based on the principle of education and self-determination among urban Black communities (Yates, 2022). In fashion, Daymond John founded FUBU (For Us, By Us), a hip-hop apparel line he funded by mortgaging his home for $100,000, and with that seed money, John rebuilt half of his home as a factory while the other half remained living space (The HistoryMakers, 2003).

Overall, with this second edition, Irvin has contributed a canonical readers' advisory source that stands alone. Just as hip-hop music and fashion have unique periods indexed in the annals of history (e.g., the Golden Age of Hip-Hop 1988–1995), so should these first and second editions be considered self-contained reference sources, needing no further updates. For anyone interested in an old-school readers' advisory sample of the street-lit genre . . . pop open this classic throwback textbook and get ya learn on!

REFERENCES

HistoryMakers, The. 2003. "Daymond John." The HistoryMakers: The Digital Repository for the Black Experience, September 16. www.thehistorymakers.org/biography/daymond-john-39.

Murray, Victoria Christopher. 2004. "Triple Crown Winner: In the Hot Category of Urban Fiction, Ex-offender Victoria Stringer Self-Published Her Story and Launched Her Successful, Independent Press." Black Issues Book Review via TheFreeLibrary.com, May 1. www.thefreelibrary.com/Triple+crown+winner%3a+in+the+hot +category+of+urban+fiction%2c...-a0116339470.

Yates, Shanique. 2022. "Master P Recalls Walking Away from a $1M Check from Jimmy Iovine—'You Gotta Know Your Self-Worth.'" AfroTech.com, March 21. https://afrotech.com/ master-p-walked-away-from-million-dollar-deal-jimmy-iovine.

INTRODUCTION
The Canonical Agency of Street Lit

More than fifty years ago, in August 1973, a Jamaican American young man known as DJ Kool Herc "broke the beat" at a street dance party in the Bronx, New York. Musical artists heard the new sound and, from that spark, told their stories with this new musical form known as hip-hop. Hip-hop culture was a sociocultural outcome of the 1970s. During that decade, freedom was being redefined in American culture as society absorbed the triumphs of the Civil Rights Movement with the passing of the Civil Rights Act in 1964. The 1970s was a time when artistic expression was abundant in Black urban life, with the emergence of reggae from Jamaica and the Black Arts Movement in the United States coalescing to redefine Black American culture. It makes all the sense that the progenitor of hip-hop, DJ Kool Herc, walks with the fused identity of Jamaican and Black American artistic culture.

Hip-hop music was infectious and spread like wildfire throughout Black America. Riding atop the waves of fluidic percussionist broken beats, hip-hop lyrics were an artistic expression of truth-telling about the realities of lived lives in urban American enclaves, predominantly housed by African Diasporic and Latino Americans, which were colloquially called "the hood." This means that hip-hop told stories with as many themes as lived in people's lives in low-income city neighborhoods: stories about love, family, and fun, as well as the complicated survival experiences of being Black and Brown in America. Thus, hip-hop became a testifying art form, giving report about the underbelly of hood living, particularly the dark side of folks navigating a violent survival economy while navigating a violent American judicial system whose ethos is based on a sociopolitical system of white supremacy. To tell the raw truth about Black stories, hip-hop emerged out of a coalescence of multiple art forms that came from the streets of urban America: emceeing (spoken word in a rhythmic rap style), DJing (facilitating music to accompany emceeing), break dancing (fluid movement to the beat), and graffiti (scribing the land/environment). These initial four elements of hip-hop coincide with elements of nature, as emceeing is the air aspect, DJing is the fire aspect (requires friction), break dancing is the water aspect (fluidity of movement), and graffiti is the earth element. And during the height of hip-hop, during the 1990s, street lit emerged as the literature that documented the stories of the coming of age of the hip-hop generation. These stories became a literary genre covering and blending various forms such as fiction, nonfiction, poetry, and biography.

In the first edition of this book, I shared my personal story of how I became a reader and advocated for the literary genre of street lit. When I was a girl during the 1970s reading at my father's feet (see first edition), these books were then known as crime novels or just simply novels, although research had been done by that time which termed these kinds of stories as "city novels" (Ault, 2006). Such research has been classified under library catalog subject headings such as "Comparative literature; Modern literature; American literature; British and Irish literature." Literary criticism abounds with ongoing explorations into the city as a setting and character for urban narratives that have conveyed the American experience from the publication of Henry Roth's *Call It Sleep* (1934), which gives a vivid insight into the Jewish American immigrant experience, to Mario Puzo's *The Godfather* (1969), depicting the Italian American early immigrant experience, to (Hakutani and Butler, 1995) to Robert Beck's (i.e., Iceberg Slim's) chronicling of urban street life of post–North Migration African Americans (Gifford, 2015).

I was a public librarian in lower-income Philadelphia neighborhoods from 1998 to 2008. When teens started coming into my library during the late 1990s and early 2000s asking for the same novels, by title and author, that were narratives about Black characters in Black city neighborhoods, I remembered my father's love for the same kinds of books. I remembered that Paul Laurence Dunbar had written a similarly themed novel, *The Sport of the Gods,* published in 1902. I recalled my readings during my African American studies classes at Rutgers University during my undergraduate years that author Richard Wright (1908–1960) had written *Native*

Son (1940) and *Black Boy* (1945) and that those novels had a raw, gritty, urban presentation to them. I then started wondering about the women writers for the Black experience in city settings. My research led me to Ann Petry's *The Street* (1946) and brought me back to revisit Ntozake Shange's poetry, *For Colored Girls Who Have Considered Suicide/When the Rainbow Is Enuf* (1977), and Lorraine Hansberry's stage play, *A Raisin in the Sun* (1959). Thus, for me, it was not a far stretch to appreciate the genre-blendedness of contemporary Black city novels/urban fiction/street lit such as Teri Woods's *True to the Game* (1994), where diary entries and poems are blended into the narrative and where many other street-lit titles included hip-hop lyrics and messaging from the new media of the day (e.g., text and social media) as part of the narrative.

As I started to research the history of these kinds of raw, gritty novels as a literary form, I learned that the genre's original name, "street literature," stems from British literary tradition dating back to the birth of the novel during the early eighteenth century, as an offshoot of compiled broadside installments from daily newspapers (the original literature talked about what was happening in the streets, sold on the streets). The term or assignation of "street lit" didn't arrive until the early 2000s, coined by library science academics (not me) who studied the reading phenomenon of urban/city novels during that time.

I remember balking at the term "street lit." I wouldn't say I liked it. I did not know where it came from or why the genre needed to be called that. Why the truncation? And why a different, separate, new(ish) name to label a genre where all the characteristics of its tradition were there (stories about the underbelly life experiences of living in the city) except for one thing: the characters in these "new novels" were Black, African Diasporic, Latinx, and LGBTQ . . . all . . . unapologetically cityfied, hip-hop, hood, and street. At the turn of the twentieth century, European immigrants had the streets talking, and their stories were being told and published as classic contributions to the American literary canon. At the turn of the twenty-first century, the descendants of Black migrants from the South, alongside a cornucopia of diverse heritages, had the streets talking in the musical form of hip-hop, translated into the literary form of street literature.

Introduction

The goal of the first edition of this book was to explain, almost justify, the literary merits of contemporary American street literature. With the current iteration of this genre, librarians, teachers, and other community-based educators seemed to be at a loss as to how to handle the stories of Black and Brown people telling their raw truths about living in impoverished city communities. For some reason, we librarians were very uncomfortable with sassy, saucy, sexy, violent, visceral stories of Black and Brown young adults and adults navigating and surviving poverty and all its requisite indicators (lack of resources, higher daily stress levels, early exposure to vices). At the same time, Daniel Defoe's *Moll Flanders* (1722) and Stephen Crane's *Maggie: A Girl of the Streets* (1893) were tucked neatly on the "Classics" shelf of public and school libraries, and V. C. Andrews's incestuously violent *Flowers in the Attic* (1979) series was merchandized on young adult (YA) public library shelves as a guilty pleasure for teen readers (I was one of those teens!).

I vividly recall my colleagues' frustration with Sister Souljah's *The Coldest Winter Ever* (1999), Teri Woods's *True to the Game* (1994), and Zane's *Addicted* (1998). I remember one library administrator yelling at me over the phone for purchasing authors Zane, KaShamba Williams, and K'wan Foye (also known simply as K'wan) to "Return those books now!" I recall colleague librarians hiding street-lit books so that teens could not have access to read them. Street lit was not just a literary problem; it was a collections problem and an information services problem with a central question: How do you perform readers' advisory (RA) for "those books"? This guide helps librarians, teachers, and other community-based educators perceive street lit as more than just being "those books" by applying RA services to meet readers' interests and information needs.

This second edition answers the call of the following goals: (1) If you are not a reader of this genre, here are some vetted titles you can read and recommend so that you can perform RA in terms of "reading what the readers read"; (2) if you want to develop your library collection with the addition of street lit, here are some suggestions; and (3) if you want or need to promote street lit in your community, here are some programming ideas.

Reader response theory has become helpful to aid librarians in appreciating that every text has its rhyme and reason, and every reader has their own aesthetic and interactive relationship with a book as story and experience (Rosenblatt, 1978, 1986; Iser, 1980). Indeed, this transactional reading experience is foundational to conducting RA: the reader has had a meaningful experience with the story and seeks out the librarian whom they trust will be interested in helping them navigate literature to read more, to think more, to appreciate and understand more, all in the quest to realize the purpose of reading in the first place, to become, more.

I began the previous edition by sharing my childhood reading autobiography. That part of my autobiographical experience came from my childhood as an inner-city Black girl growing up in the Philadelphia-Camden, New Jersey, area and from my frontline information service work as a young adult public librarian with the Free Library of Philadelphia in North Philadelphia. The introduction also recounted my first encounter with a teen patron who came to my library in 1999 asking for *The Coldest Winter Ever* by Sister Souljah. That reference interview/RA interaction was a pivotal event in my work with the genre of street literature:

One summer's day, a teen girl walked into the library, passed my desk, and veered toward the newly designated young adult area. She looked at the shelves; it was apparent she was shelf reading. She then put her hand on her hips, exhaled in exasperation, looked up and down the stack again, and then turned around as if she were looking for someone. I caught her eye, and she walked over to my desk and said:

Teen patron: "Do you have *The Coldest Winter Ever* by Sister Souljah?"
Me: "No, I haven't heard of that one, but we have her book *No Disrespect.*"
Teen: "Nah, I saw that. She's got another one now. It's really good. You should get it. For in here."
Me: "Thanks, I will. What's it about?"
Teen: "Oooh! It's about this girl who in the 'hood and she a ghetto princess, but then she loses everything, and it's like a rags-to-riches kinda story."

Me: "I'll look into getting it. We have some Bluford books—
 you wanna try out one of those?"
Teen: "Naw, those are corny."
Me: "I'ma see if I can get the new Sister Souljah for you.
 What's your library card number so I can let you know
 when it comes in?"

And that conversation was the beginning of my decades-long journey into street lit as we know it today. I do not remember the teen patron's name. Still, I can attest that the same thing that fascinated me many years ago when, as a teen, I read a bit of Iceberg Slim was a similar chord to what fascinated this young girl and was calling for her to be a reader of text and story. I could immediately relate to her excitement, interest, enthusiasm, and demand.

The popularity of street lit that occurred during the early days of the genre, arriving in public libraries throughout the United States and beyond during the Golden Age of Hip-Hop (Caramanica, 2005), raised questions about access to materials that met readers' interests and tastes coupled with librarians' reader response to twenty-first-century American street literature (Brooks and Savage, 2009; Morris et al., 2006). Since then, the genre has simmered and settled into library collections, with readership embracing digital formats (e-books) for reading.

As librarians, we must listen to what street lit has to say. As information professionals, we must learn and understand street lit's various characteristics and features as it demands its presence in the stacks. This requires us, too, to be readers of the genre (i.e., to expand how we read novels, memoirs, poetry, picture books, and graphic novels as street-lit stories), readers of our patrons (i.e., RA and outreach), and readers of our libraries (i.e., collection development, open and equal access). Thus, it behooves us to care about what patrons read: we must locate ourselves as readers along with the patrons.

As the title of this book denotes, this RA guide to street literature addresses librarians as readers of the genre. This book is also an overall readers' guide to street lit because all of us, patrons and librarians, are readers of the genre, the library, and the social interactions we participate inside and beyond library walls. This multimodal reading practice is a social literacy that simultaneously makes us readers and patrons of the libraries we serve. Thus, we are not the only experts in the stacks; patrons also have much to teach us.

This second edition has rearranged chapters to present American street literature in its proper historical, literary, and pragmatic context within professional librarian practice. This readers' guide chronicles a history of street literature to situate it along a historical, literary continuum (chapter 1), outlines the characteristics of street lit as a literary genre (chapter 2), explores the diversity of topics and themes within the genre itself (chapter 3), and offers RA (chapter 4) and collection development strategies (chapter 5). The book also articulates how we interact with the genre via library programming and outreach initiatives (chapter 6). Because a large part of my theoretical framework for my research focuses on literacy practices as forms of inquiry and reflection, I also discuss how educators, authors, and readers symbiotically participate in the reading of this genre (chapter 7). This revised second edition concludes with a new epilogue that chronicles how street lit emerged as the fifth element of hip-hop—it is a literary genre that situates the stories and lives of contemporary American city life as a solidified literary genre with its own canon.

Lastly, at the end of the book, you'll find an annotated booklist of the canon of the street-lit genre. This booklist will serve as a foundational assemblage for librarians, teachers, and community-based educators to confidently consult to build collections appropriate for their communities. This work aims to assist the American public and school librarians and teachers in understanding and appreciating twenty-first-century American street literature. Street-literature authors and readers may also find this book helpful for their research and reading interests. Resources are provided to expand collection and research possibilities.

This second edition is intended to be the final edition of this book because, from my standpoint, we don't need to continue to convince the profession that street literature is a genre, or that it is a literature that needs to be constantly explained, or that its readers' interests need to be justified ongoingly. Contemporary American street literature is a distinctly twenty-first-century genre that vividly depicts the social and economic concerns of current-day city living and survival in the United States. In this information age of social media, novels are published across various platforms: print, digital (e-books), and graphic novels. In this era of equity, diversity, and inclusion, the genre doesn't need to exist on the margins of the literary brow.

My advocacy for street lit remains solid and determined. In that vein, I am no longer interested or invested in convincing anyone of the merits of this genre or its authors and readers. During these historical times of the twenty-first century, which has become an era of reflective inquiry for every citizen, if you need to be persuaded, convinced, or impressed about the efficacy of any literary genre, that says more about one's internal biases than the morals or humanity of a genre's authors and readers.

That said, no book is ever a final draft; we don't know what the future holds for how reading interests and tastes may shift and evolve. I look forward to continued conversations about contemporary American street literature and continued learning about librarianship—the best profession in the world. Thus, as this second edition "writes back" to the first edition to solidify street lit's canonical nature, may you, the librarian reader, experience this guide with the joy of reading what the reader reads.

CHAPTER 1

History of Street Literature in American Literacy Culture

Street literature is not a new genre. Inspired by the broadsides published in Europe as far back as the early sixteenth century (Pettegree, 2017), urban street narratives have been chronicled worldwide for centuries. We are reminded of street literature in the format of broadsides, which are poster-sized newsprints with text on both sides of the paper, chronicling local neighborhood news (Shepard, 1973). Street literature has a five-hundred-year publication history in the format of broadsides and chapbooks, where ballads, poems, short stories, anthologies, and community information (ancestral "tweets") were published regularly for the reading public. During Victorian times, while the aristocracy was reading Charles Dickens's *Oliver Twist* (1837–1839) and *A Tale of Two Cities* (1859) with privileged fascination, the people whom those stories were about were reading street literature in the form of broadsides and chapbooks that sustained their authentic street culture (Shepard, 1973).

Street lit of yesteryear and today, by and large, depicts tales about the daily lives of people living in lower-income city neighborhoods. This characteristic spans historical time lines and various cultural identifications, linguistic associations, and formats. This means, for example, that a street-lit story can be from the 1800s (historical time line) about an Irish immigrant family living in the ghetto (cultural identifications), speaking an Americanized Irish dialect (linguistic associations), and rendered as a novella (format). Indeed, Stephen Crane's *Maggie: A Girl of the Streets*, published in 1893, is just such a tome.

When we consider the evolution of the broadside as a format along with its topical content of street-life narratives, poems, ballads, and adverts, we see broadsides as ephemera developed into serialized news stories and then compiled into volumes called novels (Shepard, 1973). When broadsides metamorphosed into the novel, nineteenth-century authors like Charles Dickens (*Tale of Two Cities*, 1859) and Stephen Crane (*Maggie: A Girl of the Streets*, 1893) published literary fiction to convey the uncompromising realities of American city life. During the late nineteenth century, city novels mainly focused on the ghetto lives of European immigrants in New York's slums.

Citing Crane's *Maggie: A Girl of the Streets* once more, we see a story about the brutal, impoverished daily lives of Irish residents in a New York City slum. As in today's street novels, the men in *Maggie* are characterized as frustrated, demoralized, and violent, whereas the women are depicted as melodramatic, hard-hearted, confused, and depressed. In Crane's *Maggie*, everyone is addicted to something, be it alcohol, power, or sex, and the tale (as typical in today's street lit) does not have a happy ending. Just like Teri Woods's initial publication of *True to the Game* in 1994, Stephen Crane in 1893 struggled to find a publisher for his debut novel; publishers found the text too graphic and that it "reeked of sexual realism." Indeed, publishers rebuked Crane's work:

> *Maggie: A Girl of the Streets* is a shockingly vivid portrait of the brutal conditions that existed in the poverty-stricken slums of New York. Initially refused by all publishers that it was submitted to because of its brutal and sexual realism, *Maggie: A Girl of the Streets* was first published by Stephen Crane at his own expense (back cover, Digireads.com classic edition, original publication, 1893).

Crane ultimately self-published the novel under a pseudonym. It was only after the publishing success of his classic *Red Badge of Courage* (1895) that Crane was able to publish a second edition of *Maggie* using his real name (Stallman, 1955).

MIGRATION AND SURVIVAL

During the turn of the twentieth century, unprecedented numbers of Southern and Eastern European citizens migrated to the US (Martin, 2014). This European migration wave was in its second phase, and with it came novels about the challenges people encountered in adjusting to American city life. Today, *Maggie* is considered a literary classic and a solid text in the American literary canon. Other so-called slum novels of the period that are now canonical include Frank Norris's *McTeague* (1899) and Abraham Cahan's *Yekl: A Tale of the New York Ghetto* (1896). We can also delve into British canonical literature to identify stories about survival in the streets with such titles as Daniel Defoe's *Moll Flanders* (1722), Charles Dickens's *Oliver Twist* (1837–1839), and Israel Zangwill's *Children of the Ghetto* (1892). These works helped spark a literary movement called naturalism (Campbell, 2017). We can see that street literature, as survival stories about the streets, was written to reveal the American city experiences of Irish (Stephen Crane's *Maggie: A Girl of the Streets,* 1893), Jewish (Abraham Cahan's *Yekl: A Tale of the New York Ghetto,* 1896), and Italian (Mario Puzo's *The Fortunate Pilgrim*, published in 1965 but set in the 1920s) immigrant families assimilating into American social and economic culture.

During the second phase of the Great Migration (1940–1970), when African Americans migrated from the southern US to northeast and midwestern metropolises (Smithsonian American Art Museum, 2015), Harlem Renaissance works such as Ann Petry's *The Street* (1946) and Richard Wright's *Native Son* (1940) can also be perceived as street lit. In Petry's novel, the protagonist, Lutie Johnson, is constantly fighting against the power of the street:

> Suppose she got used to it, took it for granted, became resigned to it and all the things it represented. The thought set her to murmuring aloud, "I mustn't get used to it. Not ever. I've got to keep on fighting to get away from here." . . . Because this street and the other streets, just like it would if he [her son] stayed in them long enough, do something terrible to him. Sooner or later, they would do something

equally terrible to her. And as she sat there in the dark, she began to think about the things she had seen on such streets as this one she lived in. (p. 194)

Richard Wright saw the street as a creator of consciousness. He recognized that during his lifetime, African Americans "possessed no fictional works dealing with such problems, and had no background in such sharp and critical testing of experience, no novels that went with a deep and fearless will down to the dark roots of life" (Wright, 1940, p. xvi). In his introduction to *Native Son*, in an essay titled "How Bigger Was Born," Wright shares that he learned how to apply behavioral realities of the streets to the creation of his protagonist, Bigger Thomas, by reading texts about other streets beyond US shores, specifically in London and Russia. Indeed, he said: "Actions and feelings of men ten thousand miles from home helped me to understand the moods and impulses of those walking the streets of Chicago and Dixie" (p. xvii). Wright connected the frustrations of poverty, segregation, hegemony, and injustice as a human condition commonly acted out in urban settings worldwide.

CIVIL RIGHTS

During the Civil Rights Era, works that depicted city living and survival included Claude Brown's (1937–2002) fictionalized autobiography, the now-classic *Manchild in the Promised Land* (1965) and the perennial *Autobiography of Malcolm X* (1965) by Malcolm X as told to Alex Haley. In both texts, the authors' lives are chronicled to reveal harsh realities and truths about growing up in the city and, more importantly, the challenges in successfully navigating coming of age into adulthood in low-income city environments. Additionally, more than five decades after its initial publication, the Malcolm X autobiography remains available in public libraries. *Manchild in the Promised Land* can still be found on many public and school library shelves, as its reading is often required for high schools or sought after by teen readers (Worth, 2002; Cruz, 2015; Jones, 2015).

In an obituary for Claude Brown (who died in 2002), Worth cites book critic Irving Howe's underscoring the importance of Brown's seminal work:

> What many of us talk about in abstractions . . . is here given the quivery reality of a boy's life, his struggle, his efforts at understanding. This book contributes to our sense of what America is today. (Howe, quoted in Worth, 2002, para. 4)

During the mid-1960s and 1970s, narratives such as Claude Brown's *Manchild in the Promised Land* (1965), Malcolm X's *Autobiography* (1965), and Donald Goines's two semiautobiographical series *Dopefiend* (1971) and *Whoreson* (1972) graphically and realistically depicted the harsh, gritty lifestyles of urban African Americans. There continues to be high circulation of these older street-lit titles, including titles by Iceberg Slim, who was another prolific street-lit author during the 1970s, with titles such as *Pimp: The Story of My Life* (1969) and *Mama Black Widow: A Story of the South's Black Underworld* (1969). The continuous need for public libraries to provide multiple copies of Malcolm X's autobiography as well as titles like *Monster: The Autobiography of an L.A. Gang Member* by Sanyika Shakur (1994), Nathan McCall's *Makes Me Wanna Holler* (1994), and *Down These Mean Streets* by Piri Thomas ([1967] 1997) illustrates how nonfiction is also a significant aspect of the street-lit genre.

CONSIDERING CONTEMPORARY STREET LIT

Taking all these locations for street stories into account, it is clear that the contemporary renaissance of street lit (which started in 1999) does not sit isolated on library and bookstore shelves. When we look at modern street-lit novels such as *The Coldest Winter Ever* (1999), *Dirty Game* (2007), and *Thug Lovin'* (2009), we can understand that they exist as part of a historical, literary continuum that tells similar stories in different periods. Nevertheless, they all tell stories about the street.

During the turn of the twenty-first century, street-lit authors largely self-published, marketed, and disseminated their novels. Many early titles from this time were sold literally just on the streets—on the tables of street vendors and out of the trunks of authors' cars across American cities. This entrepreneurial pattern is also historical in nature. Just as Teri Woods sold her first novel, *True to the Game* (1994), and Vickie M. Stringer sold her debut work, *Let That Be the Reason* (2001), from the trunks of their cars—we are reminded of Stephen Crane's struggle during the 1890s when he, too, had to self-publish *Maggie: A Girl of the Streets*. Authors sell their works on the streets for one primary reason: publishers reject them. Moreover, publishers have always rejected street lit for the same reasons, be it during the 1890s, the 1990s, or the 2000s: mainstream publishers considered the work too raw, gritty, graphic, violent, and sexual for the American reading public.

STREET LIT'S HISTORICAL CONTINUUM

The voices of those who live challenging lives in city enclaves use literature as a vehicle to be seen and heard. These voices depict the realism of harshly lived lives. Many literary examples exist, such as the story of a teen girl who is prostituted in the streets of London during the early eighteenth century (*Moll Flanders*), an orphan boy who witnesses horrible violence at the hand of a greedy adult gang leader of vagrant kids in the early nineteenth century (*Oliver Twist*), the short, violent interactions of an Irish family struggling to adjust to late-nineteenth-century American life (*Maggie: A Girl of the Streets*), the heartbreaking losses overcome by an early-twentieth-century Italian immigrant family able to move away from the tenements of New York City (*The Fortunate Pilgrim*), the struggles of a Harlem Renaissance single mom who is lost in the wind while trying to make a life for herself and son in Harlem (*The Street*), the deep fear and intense rage of a disenfranchised African American young adult male living in poverty in the tale of *Native Son*—street lit tells the stories of everyday people living harsh realities as they struggle to realize the American dream.

Such street survival stories continued to be published during the Civil Rights Era of the mid-twentieth century with works from Claude Brown, Chester Himes, and Malcolm X. The 1970s brought the rise of ghetto pulp-fiction novels that detailed the seedy, underworld side of city living. In the prolific works of Donald Goines and Iceberg Slim, we learn about the daily experiences of the dope fiend and the pimp as everyday people who find themselves ensconced in an underworld environment due to a lack of access to experiences beyond that environment. Goines and Slim rendered raw, gritty, realistic portraits of street life, often painting intense characterizations of drug addicts, dope dealers, and their struggles to navigate an underground economy to overcome the lure and call of the streets. Goines's and Slim's works coincided with the 1970s Blaxploitation film era, in which movies were often telling similar stories about inner-city living, with films such as *Super Fly* (1972), *Cleopatra Jones* (1973), *Shaft* (1971), and *Trick Baby* (1972), which is an adaptation of Slim's novel of the same name.

Similarly, hip-hop emerged simultaneously with the Blaxploitation and pulp urban fiction genres of the 1970s. Established on August 11, 1973, hip-hop quickly became a worldwide social and cultural force. By the 1990s, hip-hop was at a high point of creativity when, as in the 1970s, a genre of urban-focused film emerged to complement the storytelling of the urban Black experience with films by directors such as Spike Lee (*Do the Right Thing*, 1989), John Singleton (*Boyz n the Hood*, 1991), and the Hughes brothers' *Menace II Society* (1993). These films told the tales of tensions and struggles still prevalent in low-income neighborhoods. The stories are like the immigrant ghetto tales of the early twentieth century—tales of struggles with the city environment, assimilating into mainstream American culture, and coping with the daily living frustrations of various abuses (e.g., substance, physical, and street violence). Street lit emerged during the 1990s as a complement to city narratives being told in hip-hop film and music.

During the twentieth century, street lit was primarily a European immigrant story. During the early twenty-first century, the genre was mainly an African American and Latinx story, with novels about diverse African American and Latinx characters, such as Ceazia (pronounced "Cee- Asia") Devereaux, a biracial girl from an upper-middle-class background in Chunichi's *A Gangster's Girl* series (2004–2009). The ruthless gangster Dutch in Teri Woods's *Dutch* trilogy (2004–2011) fights an African drug lord to claim his empire, and alongside him is his right-hand lieutenant, the hard-knock Latina, Angel. In Black Artemis's *Explicit Content* (2004), Latina Leila Aponte and African American Cassie Rivers are best friends whose friendship is sorely tested as they ascend to hip-hop stardom. The historicity of street literature does not chronicle cultural norms or stereotypes about certain ethnic groups since it chronicles the challenging socioeconomic realities of diverse peoples, whomever they may be, who live in low-income city communities at various periods.

With time, street lit has solidified itself as a literary genre with a diverse roster of authors, titles, and formats. During this information age, street-lit authors self-publish in print, audiobook, and e-book formats. For example, Wahida Clark is a long-time bestselling street-lit author whose *Thug* series birthed Clark's publishing company, Wahida Clark Publishing, where multiple authors are sponsored alongside street-lit titles in paperback, hardcover, and e-book formats. Authors are also published by mainstream publishing houses such as Simon & Schuster, Akashic Books, Kensington Publishing, and Urban Books. Large public library systems such as the New York Public Library, Chicago Public Library, and Oakland Public Library offer all these formats plus the titles in audiobooks via OverDrive, Recorded Books, and Hoopla. Amazon.com provides a full selection of street-lit titles under the subject "urban fiction" in Kindle format.

The 1990s–early 2000s renaissance of the street-literature genre documented the historicity of city living in the late twentieth and early twenty-first century when the residents happen to be diasporic African American and Latino, with Asian and European American representation. Such diverse experiences have been documented musically in hip-hop, cinematically in various films from the 1990s and early 2000s, and literarily since the mid-to-late-1990s in street lit.

FICTION AND NONFICTION: STREET LIT ON BOTH SIDES OF THE AISLE

Interestingly, street literature comes from so many voices, spaces, places, ideas, and positions, yet the stories are all about one common theme—surviving the streets. Even nonfiction scholarly ethnographic works have been published about surviving street life and inner-city living, such as works by Elijah Anderson (2008; 2022), Katherine S. Newman (2000), Alex Kotlowitz (1992), David K. Shipler (2005), Geoffrey Canada (1995), William Julius Wilson (2009), and Sudhir Venkatesh (2006).

It should also be noted that many current-day fictional works are written by women (Souljah, Woods, Stringer, Wahida Clark, Nikki Turner, and many more). However, it seems that men write most of the nonfiction socio-anthropological works. Gender-based underpinnings exist here (Marshall, Staples, and Gibson, 2009). However, we must also acknowledge the time-honored literary preferences of women for reading fiction and men for reading nonfiction. Thus, it is not a far stretch that most street-lit authors are women and most nonfiction street authors are men. If you put the two sides of the aisle together, you have a literature collection that has always existed on personal, public, and school library shelves. What was before considered trash or risqué is now regarded as canonical.

Many poetry works speak to the street and urban experience, including contributions such as Tupac Shakur's *The Rose That Grew from Concrete* (1999), a hugely popular book in public libraries for many years after its publication. Another example of a vital poetry work that gives voice to inner-city living is Jill Scott's *The Moments, the Minutes, the Hours: The Poetry of Jill Scott* (2005). Other standard poetry works from the young adult collection that detail city realities of youths include Helen Frost's *Keesha's House* (2003), Walter Dean Myers's *Street Love* (2006), and Lori Marie Carlson's *Red Hot Salsa: Bilingual Poems on Being Young and Latino in the United States* (2005), to name a few.

History tells us that just as the nineteenth- and early-twentieth-century slum novels now hold their respectable place on library shelves as renderings of historical fiction, such will be the case for the current iterations of street literature as well. Although we may not expect such titles like *Hood Rat* (2006) by K'wan to be considered canonical based on the title alone, such a work like *Hoodlum: A Novel* (2005), also penned by K'wan, holds the possibility of standing the test of time and sitting alongside titles such as *Native Son* (Wright, 1940) or *All Shot Up* (Himes, 1960) or *Always Outnumbered, Always Outgunned* (Mosley, 1997). Sister Souljah has impacted the literary world with *The Coldest Winter Ever*, which is being read and studied in college classrooms nationwide. History also tells us that just as specific titles rose to the top of the pile to hold their place on bookshelves for decades (surely we understand that Crane's *Maggie* and Paul Laurence Dunbar's 1902 *Sport of the Gods* were not the only books of their kind published at the time), the same will happen for the street literature of today. Readers have the final say on what stays on the shelf and what does not. As librarians and educators, it is up to us to respect and honor readers' reading choices.

CHAPTER 2

Characteristics of Street Lit

Street-lit novels are stories of survival: how to survive the streets by circumventing socioeconomic pitfalls. Readers of the genre, especially teen readers who live in similar settings to those of the stories, say that reading the books teaches them "what not to do," confirms the fact that "these streets is real," and validates that "this is how it is out here in the hood" (Morris et al., 2006, p. 22). Readers outside city culture say they learn things about city living they never realized. Many readers are unashamedly, simplistically clear about why street lit appeals to them: because they enjoy reading it.

Street lit is a literary genre that centers on interpretation and representation. It provides an interpretive lens through which readers witness the survival stories of city residents living certain lifestyles. These lifestyles are varied, from the pimp and drug queen- or kingpin to the working single parent to the detective investigating a crime. Due to the mercurial nature of street lit's themes, the genre is called many things (e.g., street lit, urban fiction, hip-hop lit) and can sometimes be classified haphazardly. However, to appropriately situate street lit within the ongoing discourse on literature, with all its diversity in stories, characters, and settings, we must look at the genre from the widened lens of urbanity.

Chapter 2

URBAN, CITY, 'HOOD: LOCATING STREET LIT

There has been some debate about what to call this genre. Is it urban fiction? What does it mean to be urban fiction as compared to, say, rural fiction? Is it hip-hop lit? Ghetto lit? What do we call this literature commonly called street lit?

"Urban fiction" denotes stories set in urban settings. When we say "urban," we are talking about major cities like New York, Philadelphia, Baltimore, Chicago, Los Angeles, and New Orleans, to name a few. We are talking about major cities where the population is dense. There are urban cities worldwide—Paris, France, London, and the most metropolitan city on the planet is Tokyo (Statista, 2023). Thus, when we say "urban fiction," we are talking about a diverse range of characters and experiences that span cultural, social, political, geographical, and economic boundaries. Thus, urban fiction can encompass genres such as chick lit, lad lit, urban fantasy, speculative fiction, urban erotica, and street lit because many stories in these genres are situated in established urban settings.

Urban regions often feature neighborhood enclaves that identify with localized cultural representations. For example, many urban areas have a Chinatown or a Little Italy to denote enclaves where specific cultural groups live and thrive. Similarly, neighborhoods can be named with assignations to indicate socioeconomic status, such as saying that an enclave where poverty is prevalent is "the ghetto." Without going into the historicity of the origin and use of the word "ghetto," we all understand that in everyday, current use, the term denotes a low-income, impoverished city neighborhood. With the advent of hip-hop culture, the term "the hood" has appropriated the term "ghetto." Additionally, the term "the hood" can denote where you live, regardless of your socioeconomic status.

THE STREET AS A MOTIF

"The street" can be perceived as a character in and of itself. As a motif, the street is an aspect of the public sphere that summons, judges, and motivates citizens as they navigate life choices. In street lit, characters make decisions based on what is happening or not happening in the street. Characters often take heed of "the word on the street." This representation gives the streets a characterization with a voice; thus, the street possesses the power to inform and misinform, to command and silence characters. This street motif is inspired by real-life conceptions of the streets and what the streets can do to people and communities. Hip-hop as a culture demonstrates the streets as a powerful symbol of living life (Balaji, 2012). If I were to imagine a mathematical representation of the streets as a motif in hip-hop music, film, drama, and literature, it would be a straightforward equation: street = life. In our context for literature, we can see how street lit is indeed really "life lit."

Through many discussions about street lit in the publishing industry, various genre elements have been problematized and critiqued regarding the social, cultural, literary, and possibly moral messages that the genre voices. Scholars, educators, and authors have been debating over the years, analyzing the characterizations of women and men in street lit, the dramatic plotlines, graphic sex scenes, and violent action scenes (Chiles, 2006; McFadden, 2010; Pernice, 2010; Graaff and Irvin, 2015; Nishikawa, 2020). Even though "the streets" are referred to and deferred to as an overall theme, character, or silent antagonist of street lit, there has been no honest exploration of the symbolism of the streets or unpacking of the nuanced meanings of the streets or any thoughtful treatment of the streets as a motif for storytelling in the street-lit genre. In literature, "the street" as a literary motif is a recurring theme used to represent the setting for the story, or as a metaphor for life. For example, in *The Odyssey* by Homer, Odysseus travels along many different roads and streets on his journey home to Ithaca. The road symbolizes Odysseus's long and arduous physical and emotional journey. In *The Canterbury Tales* by Geoffrey Chaucer, pilgrims travel along the road to Canterbury. The road symbolizes life's journey, and the pilgrims' stories represent people's different challenges and experiences. In *The Color Purple* by Alice Walker, Celie spends most of her life trapped in her house and yard. When she finally leaves her home and walks down the street, it represents her newfound freedom and independence.

Chapter 2

On the blog site *Street Literature: Bringing You the Word on Street Lit and Libraries*, the street is defined as a silent antagonist:

> The street is a silent antagonist. It never speaks in language or in voice. It speaks as an expression of nature's cycles of seasons, coagulated thoughts, words, and deeds. It speaks through the gaps in silence—the exhale, the gasp before the breath—the street speaks. It demands a response to the blood it sheds, as if a sacrificial altar upon which souls are summoned to purgatory. The street positions itself as a necessary rite of passage in order to reach that American dream (whatever that may be). The street is an unnatural hell where through elevation of the mind (education) emancipation is not only possible, but inevitable. (Irvin, 2009)

The thrust of this blog posting is that the streets function as a stage in the public sphere upon which powerful and meaningful acts of community living and belonging are experienced, negotiated, and actualized.

When we say "the streets," we are talking about the actual streets that connect and intersect city neighborhoods. The streets denote territorial boundaries that define a community of residents who live in a particular area. In this vein, "the streets" is synonymous with "the hood." The streets can also be perceived as having their own identity or force that informs and influences the actions and behaviors of those who frequent, interact, and conduct business (i.e., hustle) on the streets. That is why when you read a street-lit novel, the street in and of itself is often characterized as a living, breathing entity that interacts with characters, thereby influencing and perhaps determining their decisions, activities, and fates.

As a motif, the streets symbolize possibility and the enactment of choice; it is an ominous, mysterious four-sided intersection with no directional signs. Its power is a historical pileup of diverse peoples walking, talking, sitting, lingering, playing, and observing life as it unfolds on the stage of the streets. Neighborhood residents recognize instinctively that the streets hold a wisdom, if you will, a memory of transactions and interactions that metaphysically informs those who live there. For example, the characters of Miz

Cleo and Miz Osceola in Meesha Mink and De'nesha Diamond's *Bentley Manor Tales* series (2008–2009) are depictions of inner-city residents who have survived the streets, recognize and respect their power, and sit and observe younger generations test, submit, negotiate, and reconcile with the streets.

When we think of the scene of Lutie Johnson surveying 116th Street in Harlem while looking for a place to live for her and her son in Ann Petry's *The Street* or Dutch's swagger as he walks commanding deference in his hood in Teri Woods's *Dutch* trilogy, or Jada's frustration and confusion as she wanders the streets when she leaves her mother's home to escape abuse in Tracy Brown's *White Lines: A Novel* (2007), we can see how the street is a presence but also an anthropomorphic embodiment, almost a narrator of its own scenery.

Street lit often paints the streets as this cold, fast-paced, chaotic thruway where characters fearfully and quickly move from one place to another, dodging looming dangers. In this vein, fictionalized streets accurately parallel real-life experiences. Case in point, fifteen-year-old Tony (personal names throughout are pseudonyms) admitted to his book club once that he is scared when he walks the streets in the mornings to school because he "don' know what dudes be doin' on the corners or walkin' pass me" (teen book club meeting, Philadelphia, August 2007). Another book clubber, thirteen-year-old Debbie, echoed Tony's fears, adding that she, too, is afraid when walking in the hood. Meanwhile, seventeen-year-old Cheron said it best: "You go through challenges before you even leave the house. Lotta times there's drama in the home that you gotta deal wit' before you even hit the streets."

One aspect of "the streets" as a motif is its power to converge the public (outside home) with the private (inside home). The chaos of the streets often inserts itself into unfolding dramas inside the home. The dramas in street-lit stories (fiction and nonfiction) chronicle how behavior and interactions from the streets continue to play out inside the home. Donald Goines vividly depicts one example of the streets moving into the home in his novel *Dopefiend*. In this story, the protagonist, Terry, is a middle-class working girl. At the same time, in the streets, but once inside Porky's drug house, where she begins to ingest street drugs, her inside persona seeps outside, and ultimately, as a drug addict, her private and public personas become one. When we look at street lit along a historical continuum, we see how characters' movement through the streets is often deterministic. For example, protagonists like Moll Flanders, Oliver Twist, and Winter Santiaga all experience their rise and fall in the streets.

Moll Flanders and Oliver Twist are street urchins, parentless people who come of age in the streets. For them, the fall is their tough childhood, and their rise is their coming of age. For Winter Santiaga, her rise, via her father's command of the streets because of his drug empire, confers status and prestige for her at a young age. Winter's fall occurs on the streets during her coming of age when Bullet sets her up to be arrested for drugs stashed in their car. In Will Robbins's 2009 novel *Ice*, the protagonist, Woo, comes from a fall, constantly negotiating with the streets, which is embodied in the characterization of the antagonist, Ice. Ice is the drug dealer who runs the hood. His drug runners fear and loathe him. The young runners, including Woo, work hard throughout the story to overcome Ice. Conquering Ice is the rise, equivalent to conquering the streets themselves. Conquering or surviving the streets is the overall theme of the street-lit genre. To balance the streets with life, we can say that conquering or surviving the streets is to make a success of one's life. This is the struggle that the genre depicts. It is the clarion call that it attempts to make.

FAIRY TALES AND TRADITIONAL STORYTELLING

In street lit, we see standard storytelling devices: the protagonist triad, the street as the primary stage, and characters reconciling themselves with their environments (Buvala, [2007] 2022). Whereas in fairy tales, an otherworldly kind of magic intervenes to aid characters in rising from poverty, ill health, or abusive relationships (Bottigheimer, 2009), in the reality-based tales of street lit, we have urban dwellers who must conjure their own magic through their wit, savvy, and determination to overcome the streets by way of their will. In some stories, characters may have a mentor or a guardian voice, like Ms. Blue for Precious in the novel *Push* (1996), or three protagonists will serve as support mechanisms for one another. One good example of the protagonist triad is Anne, Isaiah, and Smoke in Terra Little's *Where There's Smoke* (2009). Mother, son, and father remind one another of past mistakes and present redemptions while the parents work to keep their son from succumbing to the lure of the streets. Thus, the streets are the permanent antagonist of the genre: the streets are never glorified or sensationalized.

In street lit, the streets are the Pied Piper, the snake charmer, and the trickster of life. As such, it is something that we all must confront and deal with daily, as we use the streets as our primary path through which we work, worship, play, live, and even die. In the street-lit genre, the streets are a transformational force. Its lure, whether embraced or denied, transforms characters through life experience. Characters often descend into the nether world of the streets only to reemerge wiser, more empowered, or more hopeful for a better life (Zimmer, 2002).

In thinking about how street literature can be defined, or if it is even definable, one thing is consistent and clear: street literature is location- and setting-specific. It is a genre in which the stories, be they fiction or nonfiction, are consistently set in urban community enclaves. Settings may shift as characters travel in the stories, but basically, what makes a street-fiction story a street-fiction story is that it is set in city streets. Thus, the overall qualifying characteristic of street lit is that it is location-specific.

CHARACTERISTICS OF STREET LIT

There are eight characteristics of street lit:

- stories are location-specific, set in and depicting the livelihood of lower-income city neighborhoods
- fast-paced stories, often with flashback sequences
- vivid depictions of the inner-city environment, including lack of societal resources, substandard housing, and poverty
- the street as an interactive stage (things happen on the street or because of the street)

- female and male identity formation (via intense relationships, often romantic in nature), with protagonists often being young adults (typical age range is nineteen to twenty-five)
- navigation of interpersonal relationships, including surviving abuse, betrayal in friendships, fantastical revenge plots
- commodification of lifestyles (name-brand this, bling-bling that)
- surviving street life and overcoming street lifestyle—the challenge of moving up and away from the streets

These characteristics are not exclusive. Additional features may come and go within street lit; therefore, street-lit elements cross and blend with other literary genres, such as romance (e.g., Tracy Brown's *Black*, 2003), mystery (e.g., Solomon Jones's *The Bridge*, 2004), speculative (e.g., Zetta Elliott's *A Wish after Midnight*, 2010), and science fiction (e.g., Octavia Butler's *Mind of My Mind*, 1977). Some scholars and educators might prefer to point to more gritty themes common in street lit, such as the illegal drug trade and drug use, domestic violence, and possibly stereotypical gender-based representations of characters, as definitive characteristics of the genre.

Yet, these themes are not necessarily uniquely characteristic of street lit, as these themes occur in genres throughout Western literary tradition (e.g., romance novels, as researched in Janice Radway's 1991 *Reading the Romance*; the role of women authors in horror novels as discussed in Rafferty, 2008). Such marginalizing themes are not necessarily indicative of, or unique to, street lit. However, what is unique and peculiar to street lit is what I have determined as the overall qualifying characteristic of street lit— stories that depict realistic, naturalistic tales about the daily lives of people living in lower-income city neighborhoods. This characteristic opens our perception of street lit to include literature and formats that span life stages and cultural experiences. This overall qualifying characteristic of street lit also connects contemporary street literature with the literary tradition of naturalism, in which "characters can be studied through their relationships to their surroundings" (Campbell, 2017, para. 1) and in which there exists a tension between the interpretation of experience and the "aesthetic recreation of experience" (Pizer, quoted in Campbell, 2017, para. 4).

With these characteristics in mind, we can see how readers, especially in various city locations, are attracted to street lit. This genre tells its stories as interpretations and re-creations of scenes and activities that realistically occur in daily life. Readers enjoy reading about what they know and live. It makes readers feel competent because they are reading stories they can relate to and understand. It makes readers feel competent in their own inter-pretation of their lived life. This kind of reader response is valid for the preschooler, the school-age child, the teen, the adult, and the senior; it is helpful for the teacher, the librarian, the author, and the reader.

"IT'S LIKE A MOVIE IN MY HEAD"

Readers of young adult and adult street-lit novels have been recorded as saying, "That's not me in the story, but I know that girl. I see her walking down the street" (author's field notes, 2007). Others have said, "It's like a movie in my head" (D. Marcou, personal communication, 2009). Both statements attest to the ability of the reader to see their own reality reflected in street-lit stories but are also clear that it's not real life; it is indeed like a movie in one's head, a fiction. This idea of "a movie in the head" also speaks to the imagination being ignited while reading a street-lit story, indicating an aesthetic response to reading (Iser, 1980; Rosenblatt, 1986). This reader response attests to the genre's success in igniting reading as a literacy practice in youth and adults who were not readers.

Young adults and some adult readers have also shared that before street lit, they did not have anything to read that appealed to them that was authentic or "real." Teen readers, in particular, have stated with a tremendous sense of accomplishment that it was not until they read Teri Woods's *True to the Game* or Sister Soul-jah's *The Coldest Winter Ever* that they were able to complete a novel from cover to cover. Thus, street lit holds the power to transform reluctant readers into lifelong readers. One public librarian at a Philadelphia Librarian Book Club reflected on the appeal of street lit: "We create the street. We create the pain, the poverty, the violence. The street is a blank canvas, and we humans are the artists who have painted the picture. It is us. The street is us" (book club meeting, November 2009). Street lit appeals to readers because it offers an opportunity to investigate, validate, and make sense of the details of city life.

STREET LIT'S STRUCTURAL ELEMENTS

A street-lit novel's structure is unique for the following elements: language, format, appealing book covers, and double-entendre titles. When it comes to the style of writing, street lit has long been derided for not being well edited or well written. This was true for the earlier days of the renaissance, and it may still hold true for some entrepreneurial works that lack the benefit of a copy editor or editorial staff. However, by and large, with major publishing houses like Simon & Schuster and St. Martin's Press embracing street-lit authors and creating imprint presses to feature the genre (e.g., Dafina and Urban Soul imprints with Kensington Books), the editorial integrity of the genre has solidified.

Also, independent street-lit publishers, such as Urban Books, founded in 2002, produce quality titles that appeal to readers who have become experts in the genre. In the age of social media, readers straightforwardly demand that authors and publishers produce clean, tight, well-developed works. For example, on Amazon.com, street-lit readers are vocal in their response to novels where rankings of a title can enhance or diminish the credibility and appeal of the author. Readers may forgive the authors for their debut novel or a dud in the middle of a series. However, if subsequent publications are sloppily rendered, readers may express frustration and keenly express their expectations for a well-drafted novel. For example, one reader's comment from May 2003 on Amazon.com for Wahida Clark's debut novel, *Thugs and the Women Who Love Them* (2002), read: "This book was so bad I couldn't even finnish [*sic*] reading it. In the first story the 'pimp' character was sooooo unbelievable. It struck me more as a first draft, not a completely edited book."

Years later, Wahida Clark is now a significant author and publisher in the street-lit genre, having spearheaded her own subgenre, known as thug-love fiction, and she is colloquially referred to as the "Queen of Thug-Love Fiction." However, even after penning over a dozen titles, with one appearing on the *New York Times* Best Sellers list at one point, readers can be ruthlessly critical and demanding. Even while street-lit readers demand that stories "keep it real," they also passionately demand that authors "get it right." Case in point, sixteen readers gave Clark's seventh published title, *Thug Lovin'* (2009), a one-star (out of five stars) review. Here is what one of those customer reviewers said on Amazon.com in August 2009:

> I have no idea what book all these people [read] who said this book deserved 3, 4, or 5 stars because on its best day it's not even a 2. I waited for this book even preordered it as soon as I could. To say that I hated this book is an understatement, I feel like I was conned. . . . While reading, I kept wondering what the author's mindset was when she wrote this book, her thoughts were all over the place, and so were the characters. Events seemed out of place almost like they belonged to another story all together, and the ending made me want to scream. I will not even talk about how Trae turned into a complete asshole or how Tasha and Kyra went from being classy well educated women to, women who allowed there once lovin [*sic*] husbands to make them hoes, all in the name of revenge. The ending of the book should have been the middle, and the story should have continued from there. I see now why this book was pushed back from (publication) April 09 to August 09. If the next book in this series is as bad as this one Wahida should just hang up her crown.

Social media contributions, such as online customer book reviews, provide valuable feedback and insight into the ongoing appeal and standards within street lit and reader responses. This conveys how valuable the reader's response is in determining the direction of the genre. As of this writing, *Thug Lovin'* has received 731 customer reviews on Amazon.com, with only eighteen conferring a one-star review. However, the feedback from such low-graded reviews is an important critique that contributes to the author's relationship with their reader fan base, thus informing authors and publishers of what appeals to readers of the genre. Such reviews confirm the reality that, yes, readers demand quality literature, even from the pantheon of street-lit authors.

Language

Contemporary street lit is an African American–focused genre where most novels feature African American protagonists and antagonists and elements of African American Vernacular English (AAVE), hip-hop slang, and regional dialects. Though framed primarily around Standard American English (SAE), street lit is linguistically diverse. In addition to AAVE, elements of Jamaican patois, Haitian Creole, Caribbean Spanish, and West African languages underlie the SAE linguistic foundation, depending on the story.

Street lit authentically and unapologetically incorporates AAVE, regional dialect, and slang. The genre is written for a target audience that is literate in Black linguistic expression and can read and comprehend the form. Classic street-lit authors such as Sister Souljah, Shannon Holmes, Tracy Brown, and K'wan Foye all have employed varied linguistic forms in their literary works.

Format

Street lit can also be presented with blended literary categories. In addition to the usual prose in which novels typically occur, there are also street-lit epistolaries (e.g., Kalisha Buckhanon's *Upstate*, 2004), stories with poetry interspersed throughout the story (see *True to the Game* by Teri Woods, 1994, and *Black* by Tracy Brown, 2003), and illustrated stories (see *Midnight: A Gangster Love Story* by Sister Souljah, 2008).

Because the prevailing qualifying characteristic of street lit is location-specific, set in low-income city neighborhoods (other synonyms are the inner city, the ghetto, and the hood), we can find street-lit stories in various formats, such as poetry, picture books, and graphic novels.

There are picture books that depict city living, such as Ezra Jack Keats's 1962 classic *The Snowy Day*, in which we are introduced to the first depiction of an African American protagonist in picture books, the illustrious Peter. The question can be asked: Is this urban fiction? *The Snowy Day* is a story about Peter, about five years old, walking the streets of Harlem (alone) on a snowy day, where he makes snow angels and even realizes he is too young to participate in snowball fights. Is this street fiction? From a child's point of view, would this be a story of a successful day surviving on the streets? What about Keats's later story, *Goggles!* (1969), when Peter is older. In this picture book, Peter and his friend Archie have a run-in with a street gang.

Many picture books depict street survival—too countless to list here. However, some salient titles include *We Are All in the Dumps with Jack and Guy* by Maurice Sendak (1993), *Tar Beach* by Faith Ringgold (1996), *Brothers of the Knight* by Debbie Allen (1999), *The Neighborhood Mother Goose* by Nina Crews (2004), *My Feet Are Laughing* by Lissette Norman (2006), *Cityblock* by Christopher Franceschelli (2016), *Jayden's Impossible Garden* by Mélina Mangal (2021), and *The Year We Learned to Fly* by Jacqueline Woodson (2022), to name a few.

Many young adult titles also tell stories of the streets by authors such as Walter Dean Myers, Sharon G. Flake, Kalisha Buckhanon, and Janet McDonald, who have published many titles for tweeners. Notably, McDonald's autobiography for young adult readers, *Project Girl* (2000), is a graphic story detailing her struggles from being a ghetto girl in Brooklyn to a scholarship college girl at Vassar College, where she acquired a heroin addiction. Street-lit authors such as KaShamba Williams and L. Divine also transitioned from adult novels to publishing teen series such as the nineteen-volume *Drama High* series (Divine) and the *Platinum Teen* trilogy (Williams). These series stand on the shoulders of the pioneering twenty-two-volume *Bluford High* series by Paul Langan, which appeals to urban teen readers for its authentic depictions of navigating high school and city living.

Book Covers

The covers of street-lit novels are often full-colored depictions of young adults in urban settings dressed in contemporary streetwear. The covers may sometimes be sexually suggestive, with specific poses that suggest romance between male and female characters. The covers have been criticized for objectifying female bodily representation and glorifying misogynistic attitudes over the years (de Leon, 2019). Critics complain that with these representations, the book underscores stereotypical assumptions about urban young adults and adults as oversexualized (Thomas-Bailey, 2011; Wise, 2023).

However, some authors and publishers have moved away from this type of imagery on the book covers. For example, Sister Souljah's book covers are invariably colorful and attractive to a reader's eye. However, the imagery conveys a sense of mystery about the protagonist: Winter's eyes gaze sternly through a haze of blue and fuchsia on the cover of *The Coldest Winter Ever*. On the book covers of Souljah's *Midnight* novels—*Midnight: A Gangster Love Story* (2008) and *Midnight and the Meaning of Love* (2011)—the main character, Midnight, is depicted as a beautiful, black-skinned teen boy with a severe gaze amid a haze of the mysterious purplish hue. Teri Woods opts for bold, primary colors for her book covers, with the titles boldly displayed atop a city landscape to command attention. Her book covers rarely, if ever, feature people or faces.

Triple Crown Publications, the largest independent urban fiction publishing house from 2001 to 2010, boasted more than forty authors. The company was known for its picturesque book covers that boldly showed photogenic African American characters amid urban backdrops standing in groups to denote a multi-protagonist story, or perhaps softer, romantic poses of characters to convey a romantic tale. Patrons have been known to come into the library and ask for Triple Crown novels by brand name instead of title and author. Most Triple Crown novels were branded on the book cover with the name "Triple Crown Publications." The colorful, photographic look of the covers appeals to street-lit readers because they can relate to the urban depictions of the clothing and backdrops displayed. If readers do not remember the author or title of a book, they will often be able to convey what book they are referring to through a description of the book cover.

Titles

Book titles for street lit are often double entendres of street slang expressions. For example, Shannon Holmes's *B-More Careful* means literally "be more careful" but also denotes the locally recognized colloquial reference for the city of Baltimore, Maryland, where the story is set, as "B-More." Thus, the title also means "Baltimore careful" to convey the setting of the story and the inherent dangers of the Baltimore streets. Both meanings can be convoluted into an interwoven understanding of how to be careful on the streets of Baltimore. This kind of titling is an ingenious use of language to convey multiple meanings with few words, a signifying feature of Black linguistics and hip-hop (Gates, 2004; Haywood, 2021; Luu, 2020). Street-lit readers invariably know and understand the loaded meanings embedded within street-lit titles.

Another example comes from the foremost classic of the contemporary street-lit renaissance: Sister Souljah's *The Coldest Winter Ever*. We can take the title to mean a cold time, a span of all that the coldest winter indicates: isolation, lack (of warmth, of ease of survival, of the sun), lack of happiness and good times, survival by any means necessary. When we learn that the protagonist's name is also Winter, the title takes on another meaning to project Winter's character as icy, mean, and raw, in addition to all the characteristics of a literal coldest winter. Colloquially, in the 'hood, to be "cold" is to be cutthroat, ruthless, and heartless. Indeed, Winter Santiaga exhibits all those qualities in the story.

The double entendre is common in street-lit titles. We could also further examine *Push* (1996) by Sapphire, *Grimey* (2004) by KaShamba Williams, Quentin Carter's *Hoodwinked* (2005), Keisha

Ervin's *Hold U Down* (2006), Ashley Antoinette's *Ethic* series (2018–2019), and Dwan Williams's *Connected to the Plug* (2017) as further examples of this formulaic double-entendre titling of street-lit novels, which has proved a very effective marketing tool to appeal to readers.

CHAPTER 3

Understanding, Classifying, and Defining Street Lit

Before unpacking the diversity within today's street literature, it is essential to clarify how street lit is classified as a literary genre. Many educators (teachers and librarians), readers, authors, and publishers call street lit many things: ghetto lit, hip-hop fiction, and hood books, to name a few. However, the most common synonym for street lit tends to be the moniker "urban fiction." This is the way many educators referred to street lit when the genre gained momentum ten years ago. However, examining research surrounding this genre and its history reveals something significant: street lit is not solely urban fiction, and urban fiction is not exclusively street lit. Also, street lit is just that: a body of work that, as a genre, comes from both sides of the aisle—fiction and nonfiction.

Street lit is a literary genre of stories that are location-specific to urban/city settings. If we look at a formal definition of "urban," we can see that the word originates from, and is synonymous with, the term and idea of "city." From Merriam-Webster's online dictionary:

Main Entry: ur·ban Pronunciation: \ˈər-bən\ Function: adjective
Etymology: Latin urbanus, from urbs city Date: 1619
: of, relating to, characteristic of, or constituting a city
Source: Merriam-Webster, s.v. "urban," accessed December 4, 2023, https://www.merriam-webster.com/dictionary/urban

Chapter 3

Thus, street lit is synonymous with "urban fiction" as the title for literature set in city-based settings. "Street lit" and "urban fiction" are used interchangeably for this reason. When urban fiction is strictly confined to city-based narratives, the genre contains a few subgenres, including chick lit and lad lit (see figure 3.1).

FIGURE 3.1
Urban Fiction Subgenres

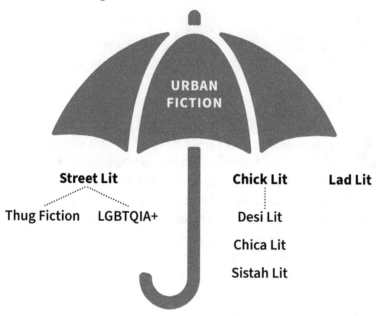

Chick lit is the female-focused genre that can be readily identified with stories such as the *Sex and the City* brand; the *Gossip Girl* series; *The Manny* (2007); and the progenitor of contemporary chick lit, *Bridget Jones's Diary* (1996; Ferriss and Young, 2005). Lad lit is a literary genre that speaks to male-focused comic stories often set in cities; the genre carries features similar to chick lit (Zernike, 2004; Jones, 2010). Leading authors of lad lit include Kyle Smith (whose 2004 novel *Love Monkey*, a male version of *Bridget Jones's Diary*, started the genre's popularity), Mil Millington, Eric

Jerome Dickey, and Nick Hornby. Notwithstanding the feminist underpinnings of chick lit and the male identity underpinnings of lad lit, when we look at all three genres—chick lit, lad lit, and street lit—their common urban backdrop gathers them all into the urban fiction genre. Urban fiction can be identified as an aspect of other genres, such as urban fantasy (e.g., Batman stories) and urban erotica (e.g., Zane).

SUBGENRES AND TERMINOLOGY

The commonality of urban fiction subgenres is the city setting. The difference between chick lit and lad lit, for example, when juxtaposed with street lit, is the socioeconomic standing of the characters. Most urban fiction subgenres are typically about characters living middle-class and upper-class urban lifestyles, whereas street lit is specifically about characters living low-income urban lifestyles. The socioeconomic condition of poverty fuels much of the action in street lit. Chick lit and lad lit stories are set in "city central," "center city," or "downtown," where metropolitan living is trendy and expensive and characters are living the proverbial American dream.

In contrast, street lit is set in "the 'hood," "the ghetto," or "the inner city," where urban living is anxiety-ridden and survivalist due to the impacts of poverty and societal marginalization. The characters are American, and in the stories, the characters seek the capitalistic American dream, too. With the characters living in a capitalistic society, consumerism is evident in the subgenres of urban fiction, regardless of socioeconomic status.

Street lit, chick lit, and lad lit also have subgenres. Specifically, with chick lit, you will find diversity within the genre with further ethnic subgenres, such as African American–focused stories, often referred to as sistah lit; Latina-focused stories, called chica lit; and Indian American stories, called Desi chick lit, to name a few. Dad lit is a memoir genre (Warner, 2007) that, though not a direct subgenre of lad lit, shows an across-the-aisle correlation between fictionalized and nonfiction men's stories.

Chapter 3

WHAT'S DIVERSE ABOUT STREET LIT?

Street lit is diverse in the stories told because the genre in and of itself is about a location-specific city population that is typically diverse. Within street lit are women's stories; men's stories; lesbian, gay, bisexual, transgender, queer, intersex, and asexual (LGBTQIA+) novels; and the popular thug fiction stories. Additionally, many nonfiction works can be considered contributions to street lit, as discussed in chapter 2.

Just as novels of yesteryear focused on the stories of low-income and working-class city dwellers who happened to be Irish (e.g., Crane's *Maggie*), Italian (e.g., Puzo's *Fortunate Pilgrim*), and Jewish immigrants (e.g., Cahan's *Yekl*), street-lit novels focus on stories about city dwellers of the same socioeconomic status who happen to be multigenerational African American transplants from the South, as well as Latino, Caribbean, African, and Asian American immigrants (e.g., Endy's 2007 *In My Hood*; Tash Hawthorne's *Karma with a Vengeance*, 2009; and Kia Dupree's *Damaged*, 2010). Some street-lit novels also depict the city experiences of whites, such as the character Molly in *Desperate Hoodwives* (2008), China in *Section 8* (2009), and even the character Skaggs in Paul Laurence Dunbar's *Sport of the Gods* (1902).

Sister Souljah's *Midnight* trilogy (2008; 2011; 2016) provides perhaps the best illustration of the diversity of contemporary city neighborhoods. The protagonist, Midnight, is an immigrant teen whose family escapes Sudan under political pressure. The family arrives in America and finds a place to live in a predominantly African American Bedford-Stuyvesant community in Brooklyn, New York. The *Midnight* trilogy is a social narrative featuring Jewish and Asian merchants and families, Jamaican American artists, Amish rural farmers, and an inside look into Sudanese-Islamic immigrant family life. *Midnight* gives us a rich depiction of the multicultural tapestry interwoven in city communities. In addition to cultural diversity within street lit, there is also gender diversity in the genre, with stories told from women's perspectives and men's perspectives, as well as a healthy contribution of LGBTQIA+ titles.

MEN'S STORIES, WOMEN'S STORIES

Street lit entails men's and women's stories that are often dramatically romantic. Characters can be found working out relationship issues from previous generations (e.g., absent parents, foster care backgrounds) or a result of their immediate environment (e.g., single-parent households, being raised in poverty). Female characters are often portrayed as passionate and aggressively in love, focusing on their femininity in terms of their outward representations (e.g., grooming, name-brand clothing, social charisma). Male characters are typically portrayed as cool and detached, navigating various levels of masculine identity construction (e.g., community status, providing for family, social prowess).

The genre does not depict women as just hapless victims of their circumstances. Female protagonists are often proactive in seeking a better life for themselves and their children, even if their modes of operation are sometimes codependent on males or misdirected into climactic events (which is what is enticing about the novels—the drama). Female characters such as Winter in *The Coldest Winter Ever* (1999), Gena in *True to the Game* (1994), and Tionna in *Section 8* (2009) are often independent, confident, and resilient. Winter has an entrepreneurial bent that proves successful when she applies herself; Gena is a romantic poet who seeks to find meaning in the happenings of her life, and her resiliency capitalizes on Tionna's loyalty and patience to survive the drama of the streets. Women's tales are often bildungsromans mixed with romance, coming-of-age stories in which the character goes through various trials and tribulations to reach a heightened sense of herself. As is true in any literary genre, with some stories in street lit, characters are successful in the end, and some are not.

Male characters tend to be proactive in their quest for respect and credibility in their communities. Male characters are often ambitious (albeit sometimes illegally so) to provide material comforts for their families and often for the women they love. Part of the machismo exhibited in street-lit stories is exhibited in the ruthlessness of drug dealing and hustling, and the ways in which men navigate relationships with enemies, legal entities, mates, and family members. For example, the character Dutch in the *Dutch* trilogy (2003; 2005; 2011) is ruthless and unforgiving in his quest for neighborhood credibility and respect from other mobsters he deals with in the established mafia. In K'wan's *Section 8* (2009; the third installment of the *Hood Rat* series), Tech is characterized similarly—as an up-and-coming street hustler demanding and commanding respect from inside and outside his world.

Family respect is vital in the portrayal of male protagonists. For example, in Terra Little's 2009 debut novel, *Where There's Smoke*, Smoke is an ex–street hustler turned high school teacher who learns he has a son. Smoke's biggest challenge is establishing a relationship with his wayward teen son to keep him away from the lure of the streets. Another novel that illustrates African American males as seeking to make a better way for themselves is *Ice* by Will Robbins (2009). In *Ice*, we learn that inner-city teen boys strive for the same things as teen boys in any other community: to graduate high school, go to college, and fall in love (not necessarily in that order). While working to graduate and attend college, Woo, the main character in *Ice*, must also reconcile himself with the streets. With the help of his father, Woo maneuvers past the feared drug lord, Ice, to avoid being ensnared by a violent street life.

Male and female protagonists like Winter, Gena, Tech, and Woo take on very human identity constructions that speak to realistic scenarios of surviving street life.

LGBTQIA+ STORIES

In street lit's twenty-first-century renaissance (the early 2000s), novels featuring LGBTQIA+ characters were published alongside mainstream street-lit titles. During the early years of the genre's popularity, LGBTQIA+ urban fiction was sometimes referred to as "homo thug" by readers. The novels featured LGBTQIA+ adult men and women (and sometimes teens) as protagonists. The stories often involved romantic entanglements that were occasionally graphic.

Works such as Asante Kahari's *Homo Thug* (2004) depict true-to-life stories of men's struggles with spending long years incarcerated, where emotional needs may be negotiated. In the

Understanding, Classifying, and Defining Street Lit

novel *Wifebeater* (a double-entendre title) by Mister Mann Frisby (2005), a homo-thug character marries the female protagonist while hiding his sexuality. Clarence Nero explores bisexuality in his acclaimed street novel *Three Sides to Every Story* (2006). In this urban drama:

> Johnny meets James, a sassy, educated drag queen from the same side of the tracks, doing time for petty theft. Worlds collide when Johnny admits to his feelings for James and becomes torn between his long-repressed homosexuality and the woman and life he had before. (From the novel's back cover)

When James and Johnny are released from prison, part of their readaptation to society is reconciling personal and family relationships.

Convict's Candy (2006) by Damon "Amin" Meadows and Jason Poole is about the realities of prison life for a transitioning teen male convicted of fraud. In this novel, Candy is a transgender person on the brink of transitioning from male to female when convicted and sent to federal prison. While in prison, she faces myriad relationship issues. The novel is also a social commentary on HIV/AIDS in communities.

Another title that features a transgender protagonist is A. C. Britt's *London Reign* (2007). *London Reign* features a teen protagonist, a boy trapped in a girl's body. In this story, London is a severe street hustler who is also coming of age with her emerging identity.

Many street-lit novels feature lesbian, bisexual, transgender, and questioning characters. Some titles include *Love Lockdown* by Mia Edwards (2010), in which the character Rasheeda is a powerful lesbian drug lord who, through the protagonist's half-sister Tiffany, holds sway over the fate of the protagonist, Kanika. In *Dutch II: Angel's Revenge* by Teri Woods (2005), Angel is a lesbian whose ruthlessness has her involved in a fair number of intense affairs to reach her criminal goals, whereas *Strapped* by Laurinda D. Brown (2007) features the character Monique Cummings, who adopts a masculine hustler identity to take control of her own life. Additionally, *Trickery* by Christine Racheal (2010) is about

Taj, a lesbian sex performer who plays a dangerous game with her sexual identity, eventually revealing her secrets. Of notable mention is the author N'Tyse, whose novel *My Secrets Your Lies* (2007) is an adventurous tale about a lesbian couple, Sand and Rene, who cut their teeth on the streets as hustling teens and grow as a couple into their brand as adults. While Sand seeks to legitimize her business, the long-term relationship begins to wane for Rene, who is questioning her gay identity. A significant theme in the story is how Rene branches out to explore her identity in a heterosexual relationship.

All in all, LGBTQIA+ novels follow the same main theme of the umbrella genre of street lit: surviving street life while navigating relationships. Although LGBTQIA+ titles may not be heavily published within street lit, for interested readers (especially LGBTQIA+ teens), this subgenre can serve as a gateway to a thriving LGBTQIA+ genre that features authors like Clarence Nero and Laurinda D. Brown, as well as Michael Warren, Cheril Clarke, and E. Lynn Harris.

THUG FICTION: KEEPING IT REAL

Thug fiction is a subgenre of street lit that author Wahida Clark dominates. With titles like *Thugs and the Women Who Love Them* (2002), *Thug Matrimony* (2008), *Justify My Thug* (2011), and *Thugs: Seven* (2019), Clark is the undisputed progenitor of the "thug" street-lit subgenre. Clark is an *Essence* magazine bestseller; the second installment of her seven-volume *Thug* series, *Every Thug Needs a Lady,* appeared on the *New York Times* Best Sellers list shortly after its 2006 publication.

While the traditional definition of a thug is "criminal" or "gangster," within the context of street lit, there is a cultural (in terms of the streets) definition that is more about surviving street life than about being a criminal. The top definition at the website Urban Dictionary cites the rapper Tupac Shakur (1971–1996):

> As Tupac defined it, a thug is someone who is going through struggles, has gone through struggles, and continues to live

day by day with nothing for them. That person is a thug. [A]nd the life they are living is the thug life. ("Thyung", Urban Dictionary, 2005)

Thus, being a thug is about how one successfully copes with intense daily life issues that are typically exacerbated by poverty and societal marginalities. Coming from an urban and decidedly hip-hop context, "thug-ism" is about how one successfully copes with daily navigation of the streets. What is indicative of thug fiction is how couples love and commit to each other (e.g., the infamous Wahida Clark characters, Trae and Tasha) despite poverty and the perilous violence of the streets. Thug fiction directly focuses on the romantic and erotic experiences of couples, and as a result, it can be thought of as the romance subgenre of street lit. What differentiates thug fiction from traditional romance fiction is the grittiness of the stories and, again, the geographic commonality of the city streets as the staged backdrop for the stories' action. Another feature of thug fiction is commitment: Wahida Clark (and her cadre of authors) does not write one novel, and the story is done. She writes her stories as a series, where characters' lives are deftly interwoven with one another to learn hard life lessons. Clark punctuates the point:

> Thugs do love, and they can love hard. In *Thugs and the Women Who Love Them*, Faheem gives up his love of the drug game just to win Jaz's heart, who was his real love. Yes, thugs do commit. Street-running Trae and Kaylin married and fell deeply in love with Tasha and Angel. You reap what you sow, or what goes around comes around, is the underlying message in all of my books. You receive the reward or the punishment as a consequence of what you do. This makes my books, the "thug love" genre, different from street lit. (W. Clark, personal communication, June 9, 2010)

Clark's *Thug* series begins with one set of characters in the first novel and then continues in subsequent installments to include and highlight friends of friends and foes in the subsequent books. If you are a loyal reader of the *Thug* series, you become ensconced in the fictional world that Clark creates because you, as the reader, become invested in what happens with the characters. Case in point, one customer reviewer commented on Amazon.com in response to reading Clark's *Thug Lovin'* (2009): "The magic of books 1–3 is the message that our [African American] powerful connections do exist (contrary to what the media would say) and that they are to be celebrated" (Amazon customer review, "Indigo," August 4, 2009).

Wahida Clark is a prolific author and publisher of multiple series that total twenty-seven volumes. Her collaborative approach to publishing multiple authors within her series has ensured Clark a loyal readership and plenty of space to develop authentic characters. In this vein, thug fiction maintains the very essence of street lit: keeping it real.

STREET LIT VS. URBAN EROTICA

Street lit and urban erotica are often conflated; however, it is essential to understand that the two genres are distinct literary traditions that happen to attract the same readers. Street lit is location-specific, whereas urban erotica is not—its stories take place in settings from various geographies and socioeconomic loci. The romantic lens of street lit primarily comes from renowned author and publisher Wahida Clark's brand of street lit known as "thug fiction," which can be considered a blend of street lit and urban erotica, as the subgenre carries elements of the inner-city setting from street lit and the romantic drama from urban erotica.

The differentiation between urban fiction/street lit and urban erotica is essential to note because both genres feature the city as the main setting and focus on the lives of people living in low-income city neighborhoods. Both genres are often characterized by their fast-paced plots, vivid descriptions of urban life, and strong female characters. Both urban fiction and urban erotica often explore themes such as poverty, crime, violence, drug use, sex, and love. These themes are often explored in a realistic and gritty way. However, urban erotica focuses on depicting sexually explicit content as escapism and fantasy. In contrast, while focused on romance and the complexities of relationships, urban fiction primarily tells stories that explore social issues such as poverty, crime, and violence.

Today's street-lit stories have a central theme in common with urban fiction stories of yesteryear: navigating relationships within the circumstances of poverty, where relationships are a primary lens to the story, from Charles Dickens's *Oliver Twist* to Sister Souljah's *The Coldest Winter Ever*. Along the historical continuum, street-lit stories focus on relationships with characters experiencing interpersonal conflicts they seek to navigate and overcome. Everyday citizens are characterized as having to reconcile unavoidable fates with street life and then struggling to either conquer or surrender to the streets' will.

CHAPTER 4

Readers' Advisory
Approaches to Street Lit

R eaders' advisory for street lit requires the librarian to care about the genre, but more importantly, to care about the patron. Reading is ultimately a private, personal endeavor. Thus, when patrons come to the library to seek a librarian's guidance on their reading interests, that interaction is intrinsically embedded with a vulnerability that requires an immediate reciprocity of trust.

Because street lit is often regarded as transgressive and controversial, this trust factor is imperative for a successful readers' advisory interview between the patron seeking advisory on street lit and the librarian. Librarians must be aware and sensitive to the fact that when patrons, particularly patrons seeking this genre, come for professional assistance, they are essentially the experts of their preference (i.e., they invariably know what they are looking for) and are purposefully seeking the librarian's support. Thus, that support should be professional, which means it must be packaged with a nonjudgmental and open-minded attitude. Often, patrons seek the librarian's professional assistance because they have acquired the reading habit from reading the genre and want to read something new.

Patrons come to the librarian with the expectation that the librarian is knowledgeable about the genre (or, at the very least, their library's collection) and is competent (socially and intellectually) to recommend good, reputable titles with a competency-based approach to readers advisory (Smith, 2000; Van Fleet, 2008; Evans, 2019; Abdul, 2022). Librarians should also keep the American Library Association's *Code of Ethics* (2021) and the Reference and User Services Association's *Guidelines for Behavioral Performance of Reference and Information Service Providers* (2023) in mind when working with patrons for readers' advisory.

Many people of all ages and backgrounds read street lit; city, suburban, and rural teens read street lit. Many adults, including addiction rehabilitation clients, read the genre and may read street-lit novels as bibliotherapy (Aiex, 1993; Verden, 2012; Cannon, 2018; Zanal Abidin et al., 2023). I can attest to working with addiction rehabilitation clients in Philadelphia and referring them to Donald Goines's and Iceberg Slim's novels for this purpose. Addiction rehabilitation clients may also enjoy novels by the classic street-lit authors K'wan Foye, Ashley and JaQuavis Coleman, and Teri Woods, to name a few. As teens have reported that they enjoy reading street lit because it teaches them what not to do (Morris et al., 2006; Guerra, 2012), adult readers rehabilitating from addictions acquired from street living may read the genre for the same reason.

Although many adults read street lit/urban fiction for entertainment, teen readers often consume these volumes not only as entertainment but also to make sense of the confusion that permeates their communities. Living in poverty in America is far from the mainstream, middle-class narrative depicted in the global media as the American dream (Compton-Lilly, 2007; Saffou, 2014; Lyubymova and National Linguistic University, Kyiv, Ukraine, 2021). People unfamiliar with American city life often struggle to accept that these fictionalized depictions of life in the 'hood could so closely parallel the daily realities that many Americans face; however, my fieldwork in teen readership of street lit confirms that the genre is primarily based in a world that the readers recognize as real. As one book club reader, Angie (age sixteen), stated: "It's reality for me." Another clubber, eighteen-year-old Tanya, said: "It's all life; non-fiction, fiction. It's life." With American street-lit novels typically set in major metropolitan areas such as New York City, Atlanta, Los Angeles, Philadelphia, and Baltimore, teen readers often see themselves or someone they know (a friend or relative) within a narrative. Such recognition empowers them to make sense of their lives (Morris et al., 2006; Morris, 2007; Kumasi, 2010; Gibson, 2016).

Indeed, as Lily Owens (1981) wrote in *The Complete Brothers Grimm Fairy Tales*, characters in oral fiction and folktales based on a parallel reality allow us to understand reality further: "however high or low, exaggerated or outlandish, the emotions and experiences of fairy-tale characters have their real-life counterparts. . . . [We are] recognizing our world in theirs" (p. xiv). There is a connection between the worlds depicted in street-lit novels and the worlds that lower-income teens in cities and rural communities navigate daily. The challenges of living in low-income homes and low-resourced neighborhoods have teens experiencing unique obstacles in their communities. Because teens navigate these obstacles at the most intense developmental stage of their lives (i.e., adolescence), how they perceive their worlds is more intense and amplified (Dimitriadis, 2003; Anderson, 2022).

To map the connection between the worlds of street lit and real-life city worlds, we must place ourselves in readers' shoes to comprehend their localized narratives (Sumara, 1996; Barton and Hamilton, 1998). This may not be an easy or attractive option. Public educators (librarians and teachers) serving today's American citizenry must often accept that many students live and operate in the same visceral conditions as the environments described in street-lit novels. Confrontation with this truth is necessary to understand why teen readers gravitate toward stories that parallel their lived experiences rather than escaping into the polarized realities of other forms of literature.

READERS' ADVISORY FOR TEENS

Because there is a significant teen readership of contemporary street lit, librarians must be attuned to adolescent developmental information needs that pertain to literacy activities that are text-based as well as social (Chance, 2008; Gorman and Suellentrop, 2009; Agosto, 2022). Teens' information needs are best met when the librarian respects their choices and encourages critical analysis as part of their journey to becoming information literate. For example, if a teen comes to a librarian asking to read *Section 8: A Hood Rat Novel* or *Thugs and the Women Who Love Them*, it behooves the librarian to approach the query thoughtfully, considerately, and empathetically. The librarian's regard for teens' reading tastes and practices can significantly affect readers and determine their lifelong engagement with reading and libraries.

Even though the patron may seek readers' advisory to learn what is available in the library, it is not the librarian's place to shuffle the patron to other literary genres or other Black or Latino authors who may be more palatable to the librarian's personal reading tastes. It is also not advisable for the librarian to thoughtlessly whisk the patron to the "Black section" of the library to dismiss the patron and avoid having to engage in the interview. Librarians avoid becoming familiar with the street-lit genre at their professional peril, as patrons request it in urban, rural, and suburban libraries. It is best if librarians understand the genre from a historical perspective so that they are fortified with the understanding that the current iteration of the genre is cyclical yet comparable to other fiction works that are now considered canonical (see chapter 2). To come to a well-rounded understanding of street lit as a genre, librarians must approach the genre with respect for its historicity and cross-pollination with other genres.

It is necessary to note that during the early days of the rise of contemporary street lit (1997–2008), teen readers' consumption of adult street lit did prompt cries of foul play from educators who identified that some themes, language, and scenarios were too mature for younger readers. Indeed, readers as young as twelve have been known to read novels like Sister Souljah's *The Coldest Winter Ever* (1999) and Kiki Swinson's *Wifey* (2004). However, street-lit authors spearheaded a softer, toned-down version of street lit for tweeners, thus igniting a much-needed publishing revolution for the African American and Latino young teen and tweener reading public. Specifically, teen-friendly street lit was made popular by author KaShamba Williams.

TONING IT DOWN FOR TWEENS

When I was an adult/young adult librarian, I attended an author event at the Overbrook Park Branch Library in Philadelphia, where the street-lit author KaShamba Williams was the featured guest, where she was promoting her novels *Blinded* (2003), *Grimey* (2004), and *Driven* (2005). During the program, Williams shared her story about her twelve-year-old daughter (at the time) wanting to read her novels, to which she replied, "Absolutely not." Williams conveyed that it was at that point that she realized the necessity of publishing a teen-friendly street-lit book for a younger reading audience. Soon after, she announced the upcoming *Platinum Teen* series and four novels were published: *Dymond in the Rough* (2005), *The Absolute Truth* (2005), *Runaway* (2006), and *Best Kept Secret* (2008). Author KaShamba Williams was the first author to pen and publish a teen-friendly street-lit brand with the defunct Precioustymes Entertainment Publishing company (2003–2008). Williams's brand spearheaded an evolution in publishing for city tween audiences, with authors such as L. Divine, the Kimani Tru conglomerate, Coe Booth, Paula Chase Hyman, and Kia Dupree realizing literary success in this area.

Teen-friendly street lit intends to offer the stories of city living and struggle without the graphic language, violence, and sex scenes of adult street lit. The stories target tweeners (twelve to fourteen) and younger teens (fourteen to sixteen). Although we can look to the ever-popular *Bluford High* series as well as established young adult (YA) authors such as Sharon M. Draper, Angela Johnson, Sharon G. Flake, Janet McDonald, and Walter Dean Myers, who have been writing teen-friendly urban novels with a city focus for years, KaShamba Williams's *Platinum Teen* series signified a turn in YA publishing for the urban teen reading audience. What was significant about Williams's series was that the book covers displayed full-bodied pictures (not graphics, headshots, or silhouettes) of contemporary, relatable African American tweeners and teens, along with double-entendre titles that mirrored the representation of adult street lit. Also notable about Williams's series is that she branded the book covers as "teen-friendly street lit."

The works of Sharon G. Flake and Walter Dean Myers are significant representations of teen novels that chronicle realistic city stories. We can appreciate the artistry that Flake, Myers, and other African American authors of YA novels exhibited in the works that garnered them literary awards, such as the first Michael L. Printz Award for Myers's *Monster* (1999) and Flake's multiple Coretta Scott King Awards and honors. However, Williams's *Platinum Teen* series was vital to YA literature because it was written in a simple, straightforward dialectal language, laced with slang and contemporary terms that translated into fast-paced stories that tweeners and young teens readily related to. Tween readers enjoy the sense of accomplishment of reading stories with characters that continue to evolve in installments, as opposed to storylines that are one-time reading experiences.

Salient Teen-Friendly Series

What ensured the success of the teen-friendly street-lit series was the same entrepreneurial approach that engineered the success of adult street lit—self-publishing and packaging (or branding). KaShamba Williams self-published the *Platinum Teen* series and packaged it with colorful, photographic book covers and double-entendre titles. By offering installment stories instead of stand-alone novels and realistic, relatable stories, a more African American–focused teen-friendly street-lit series emerged with significant readership: *Drama High* series, which L. Divine spearheads. Set in California, the series focuses on the teen protagonist Jayd Jackson, who navigates her life between the ghetto of Compton, California, and attending high school in a white Los Angeles suburb. Divine engages with her teen readers via her Facebook, Twitter, and Instagram social media accounts. She adds updates on her publications, shares reader photos, and responds to reader questions. The series' target audience is ages fourteen and up.

Darrien Lee, an *Essence* magazine best-selling adult street-lit author, pens the *Denim Diaries* series. Boasting six volumes, the series chronicles a teen protagonist, sixteen-year-old Denim Mitchell. We follow Denim's roller-coaster life as she and her diverse group of friends experience first loves, school drama, and increased responsibilities at home and beyond. Lee's storytelling balances the issues of the streets with realistic parental presence. The series attracts boy and girl readers alike (and their parents) and is nicely packaged with photographic book covers.

The *Bluford High* series was originally published by Paul Langan of Townsend Press in 2002, with artistic drawings of African American characters as the book covers. In 2006, Townsend partnered with Scholastic Press to reissue and repackage the series with contemporary photographic book covers depicting African American teens. Townsend engages with *Bluford High* readers via a Facebook page, which updates readers on upcoming titles, answers questions, and moderates discussions on a reader discussion board. The *Bluford High* series' target audience is middle school tweeners ages twelve to fourteen.

The *Kimani Tru* series was independently published in 2006, with eleven volumes published in 2007. Since 2007, the series has been an imprint of Harlequin Books. Authors Monica McKayhan and Earl Sewell are frequent contributors. *Kimani Tru* titles are geared toward readers sixteen to twenty years of age.

The *Fab Life* series was published from 2010 to 2013. It is popular with older African American teen girls and is suitable for school library collections. Penned by Nikki Carter, there are six titles, including *Not a Good Look* and *All the Wrong Moves*. The *So for Real* series is another popular series by Nikki Carter. Published in 2009–2010, this series contains four titles targeted at middle-school-age readers.

Author Ni-Ni Simone has several series focusing on the teen city living experience: *Ni-Ni Girl Chronicles*, *Hollywood High*, and *Throwback Diaries*. Published from 2008 to 2018 with a total of eleven installments, the narratives of the Ni-Ni Simone series explore the intersections between social issues and the teen angst that many teens face, offering insight into relationships, self-esteem, and body image with an optimistic view on everyday life. Simone interweaves her characters throughout the installments, where different stories from the same neighborhood are featured in various titles. Simone maintained a Facebook fan page until 2018 where she engaged with her teen readers. On the page, teens communicated about their reading experiences, favorite characters, and how they learned a love of reading from reading her books. One teen posted in 2010: "ive read all the books, and ive hated reading but ever since i read your books ive loved reading lols."

Teen-friendly street-lit series ushered in a movement in YA publishing to meet the reading interests and needs of urban African American tweens and younger teens. Had it not been for street lit and its interpretation of African American city life, YA publishing would not have experienced the renaissance for African American–focused series fiction that it has, which filled the much-needed gap in literary series for African American teen readers. In more recent years, authors such as Angie Thomas, with her award-winning novel *The Hate U Give* (2017), have continued to tell the story of the real-life experiences of African American teens confronting social, economic, and cultural challenges in the forms of struggling relationships, societal discrimination, and racial violence.

Christian Teen-Friendly Series

A further outcome of teen-friendly street lit is the emergence of Christian-themed series for the urban, African American teen reading audience. There are many Christian-focused teen-friendly series for urban African American teen readers. These titles are often geared toward the twelve-to-fourteen and fourteen-to-sixteen age groups. Stephanie Perry-Moore is perhaps the most prolific of the Christian series writers. Her titles include the following: *Beta Gamma Pi* series (ages fourteen to sixteen); *Carmen Browne* series (ages twelve to fourteen); *Yasmin Peace* series (ages twelve to fourteen); *Payton Skyy* series (ages fourteen to sixteen); and *Perry Skyy, Jr.* series (ages fourteen to sixteen).

ReShonda Tate Billingsley writes the *Good Girlz* series (ages fourteen to sixteen), Victoria Christopher Murray heads the *Divas* series (ages fourteen to sixteen), and Jacquelin Thomas pens the *Divine* and the *Divine and Friends* series (ages fourteen to sixteen).

These Christian series are often set in urban settings with African American teen characters navigating home life, social romances, and personal struggles resolved with prayer and applying religious principles. These series also fill a significant gap in Christian teen fiction. Whereas YA literature was replete with works such as the *Left Behind* series (sixteen volumes) by Tim LaHaye and Jerry B. Jenkins and the *Diary of a Teenage Girl* series (multiple iterations: Caitlin, Maya, Chloe, Kim) by Melody Carlson, it was missing an African American presence within this literary tradition. The emergence of street lit inspired a (re)turn to African American–focused Christian fiction as an alternative to tweeners and young teens reading adult-oriented street lit.

As we all know, literature comes in various textures and flavors to meet all kinds of readers' reading interests and needs. Readers have degrees of sensitivity, from reading graphic stories like horror or supernatural fiction to reading sexy stories like urban erotica (e.g., Zane) and contemporary romance. In teen-friendly street lit, the same holds: some tweeners and teens are sensitive to reading teen-friendly street lit, and some older teens can handle adult/young adult (A/YA) street lit. Teen-friendly street-lit novels, series, and Christian works are not meant to act as censorial substitutes for contemporary A/YA street lit. There will be teens whose sensitivities and interests will lean toward teen-friendly street lit, and there will be teens who will request modern A/YA street lit. Both audiences should be equally respected with a comprehensive collection to meet their reading and information interests and needs.

It is understood that school media centers tend to have more rigid collection development policies. Teen-friendly street lit can be an excellent compromise for developing middle and high school collections with compliant street-lit stories. Authors such as Coe Booth, Paula Chase Hyman, Todd Strasser, Paul Volponi, Alan Lawrence Sitomer, and Allison van Diepen offer teen-friendly street-lit novels appropriate for public and school library collections. Classic works that have stood the test of time and critique (e.g., *Manchild in the Promised Land*, *The Coldest Winter Ever*) are good additions to a high school library collection. Nonfiction memoirs and biographies, such as the *Autobiography of Malcolm X*, are also valuable additions.

Chapter 4

"KINDA SORTA BUT NOT STREET LIT" YOUNG ADULT TITLES

There are a few authors who write novels that are teen-friendly and set in urban contexts that may appeal to readers who have exhausted your collection. The following authors' debut novels received good responses from readers and educators:

Zetta Elliott's *A Wish after Midnight* (2010) is a speculative fiction novel about fifteen-year-old Genna, an Afro-Latina from the Brooklyn projects who unexpectedly goes on a time-travel adventure to her same neighborhood during the US Civil War. The novel is historically accurate and has received good reviews for being an engaging read.

Tachelle Shamash Wilkes's *Amanda's Ray* (2010) is a teen-friendly urban narrative about Amanda, a talented writer and lyricist, who is starstruck by a female rap star and wants to be just like her. An unfortunate event lands Amanda in a juvenile detention center, where she goes through a downward identity crisis because she is obsessed with contacting her celebrity muse. Amanda comes full circle to realize that she is the real star; all she has to do is look within. Readers have lauded this novel as an inspirational read.

Dia Reeves's debut novel, *Bleeding Violet* (2010), can be considered a dark fantasy novel for the A/YA reader age sixteen and up. Sixteen-year-old Hanna is a biracial girl who tries to reconnect with her mother, who abandoned her. To be able to stay in her mother's home, Hanna must settle in with new friends at the local high school. This is not an easy feat for a manic-depressive girl who experiences hallucinations. However, given the haunted nature of her town, Hanna learns that her unusual, sometimes violent nature is compatible with this new community's paranormal weirdness. A demon-hunting group quickly recruits her and goes on a quest to save the town from dark evils. This novel can be considered a hybrid of horror and mystery—it has sex, violence, and some gore.

Thug fiction queen Wahida Clark started the YA imprint Wahida Clark Presents Young Adult in early 2011, with the debut of Rashawn Hughes's novel *Under Pressure*. The narrative features

Quentin Banks, who is comfortable with his swagger on the streets of the Bronx. Eventually, "QB" spends some time in prison, but on release, he returns to his Bronx neighborhood to do good in the world. Older and much wiser, QB becomes a youth counselor at a local teen community center—QB mentors two young men, Torry and Chase. When a showdown targeting QB for an old beef occurs, QB struggles to quell his instinct for revenge. *Under Pressure* is a coming-of-age story that may appeal to teen male readers. Warning: Some graphic elements in the novel may be too mature for readers younger than sixteen. Clark has published several YA titles that are milder in content to appeal to a broader range of teen readers. In addition to *Under Pressure*, girl titles include author Gloria Dotson-Lewis's titles *Ninety-Nine Problems* (2011) and *You Got Me Twisted* (2018), and Charmaine White's *The Boy Is Mine: A Wilson High Confidential* (2018).

THE VALUE OF TEENS READING STREET LIT

Even before inner-city children reach their teenage years, most are profoundly aware of their environments. Having worked with inner-city teens for nearly a decade (and having grown up as one myself), I have seen how street lit aids in teens' overall comprehension of their surroundings. These teens of the hip-hop generation have learned to combine urban literature (street lit) and music (hip-hop) to empower themselves. Looking at life critically to "know what's going on" is vital to today's teens' survival, and street lit plays an essential role in not only heightening their resistance to any unsavory people and locations surrounding them but also strengthening their resiliencies, thus allowing them to carve out a sober space within their neighborhoods.

Street lit benefits its teen readership by bringing value to their worlds and points of view. As my fieldwork has revealed, teen readers regularly incorporate the novels' themes into their daily responses to their environment in hopes of learning what not to do (Morris et al., 2006). To coin Kenneth Burke's phrase, as cited by Elizabeth Long (2003) in *Book Clubs: Women and the Uses of Reading in Everyday Life*, teens use street lit as "equipment for living" (p.

131). Thus, although the books may not be written for that specific purpose, teenage book club members show that teens often interpret the novels as cautionary tales, and the more of the genre they read, the more critical they become of their future readings.

Reflection, Analysis, and Connection

Consistent reading of the genre is creating an outcome of inner-city teen readers gaining both critical analysis skills about their reading tastes and, by extension, heightened understandings of their communities. Because adults predominantly write street-lit novels, these authors often report back to their cultural communities to document their experiences in history and to warn of the perils of bad choices regardless of one's environment. With these novels, the authors seek a consensus from their readers, by which readers affirm the authors, who are thus reconciled from their past wounds. To perceive street-lit books as acts of contrition illustrates an ongoing conversation and a mutual inscriptional discourse between author and reader (Iser, 1978; Rosenblatt, 1983; Appleyard, 1991; Sumara, 1996). New beginnings occur when you remember the past and the present and bring both into the future (Lavenne, Renard, and Tollet, 2005; Hua, 2006). This chaotic process creates opportunities to move the African American ghetto culture and community forward. Although some insiders and outsiders to inner-city living may not endorse the lifestyles depicted in the dramatic scenarios of street-lit novels, it is essential to recognize the genre's effect on students, including one fourteen-year-old ninth-grader who wrote in a teen survey I conducted in 2008, "[For teens] there are a lot of things going on in the world, and we need to be involved."

Developing a Sense of Self

Because the teenage years mean that a child is in the process of articulating their identity and because inner-city students must often navigate the added stress of their intense and unpredictable communities, I submit that inner-city teens seek the validation that street literature provides because reading the stories suggests that they can gain control of normalized anxieties and uncertainties and make changes in various aspects of their beliefs and understandings.

Reading street lit allows teens to claim some ownership over their daily lives by comparing their realities and identities to the characters in these folk stories. Street lit gives teen readers a sense of being proactive, allowing them to slow down to examine and process the rise and pitfalls of ghetto life. By taking their time to contemplate the world in which they live, the teens, as readers, have a chance to decide, "This is not me; these are just the circumstances of my life right now. This is just my current world, my current reality, but it is not the reality I want to live."

SEARCH TERMS AND KEYWORDS

When embarking on a readers' advisory interview, librarians often go to an online public access catalog (OPAC) or the internet as their first access point for searching for titles. In the earlier years of the street-lit renaissance (1998–2004), it was challenging to find the books in library catalogs because they were categorized differently based on location (e.g., "Baltimore (Md.)—Fiction") and ethnicity (e.g., "African Americans—Fiction"). During 2008 and 2009, when I was working collaboratively with the Library of Congress (LOC), "urban fiction" was added as a subject heading to the Library of Congress classifications (I. Quitana, personal communication, October 21, 2009).

Street-Lit Keywords and Search Terms

Keywords and search terms that can be used for locating street lit via an OPAC include but are not limited to "urban fiction," with the following cross-references:

- crime fiction
- gangster fiction
- hip-hop fiction
- inner cities
- organized crime fiction
- street fiction
- street life
- street life fiction
- street lit
- urban life

All these subject headings can be used as search terms to search web resources such as Goodreads, Amazon, and Libby, where readers tag books they read and provide comments and reviews.

Often, patrons will enter the library knowing the book title or theme they seek. Often, they will also know the author's name and the publishing brand (e.g., Bluford, Holloway House, Urban Books). Additionally, many books are independently published or published by smaller outlets. Thus, some titles may have the requisite International Serial Book Number (ISBN) for cataloging purposes but lack a full Machine-Readable Cataloging (MARC) record.

READERS' ADVISORY QUESTIONS

Questions that could be posed to patrons would be directed to the following access points: setting, story, relativity, and authenticity. Based on these access points, when performing readers' advisory for street literature, use questions that point to what appeals to readers. See the following sections for some suggested questions.

Setting

Q: Is there a particular city or neighborhood you want to read about?

As a location-specific genre, street lit is often set in large metropolitan cities such as New York, Philadelphia, Oakland, and Atlanta. Some novelists write stories about a particular region. For example:

- Teri Woods, Solomon Jones—Northeastern: Philadelphia
- K'wan, Relentless Aaron, Sister Souljah—Northeastern: New York City
- Kiki Swinson, Nikki Turner—Southern: Virginia, Baltimore, D.C.
- Quentin Carter, Keisha Ervin—Midwestern: Kansas City, St. Louis
- Renay Jackson—Western: Oakland

Patrons may want to travel to another location, or they may want to read about a familiar place. Either way, the librarian needs to be familiar with the geographical patterns of the genre, as the genre is setting-focused and location-specific.

Story

Q: Do you like mysteries? Romance? Fantasy, science fiction, or speculative fiction?

Street lit features elements of other genres:

Mystery: For example, Teri Woods's novels are crime capers, so mystery readers may be interested in her works as well as titles such as Solomon Jones's *Ride or Die* (2005), Meesha Mink's *All Hail the Queen: An Urban Tale* (2015), or Kiki Swinson's *Public Enemy #1* (2021), to name a few.

Romance: The most famous romantic couple in street lit is Gena and Quadir, the protagonists of the *True to the Game* trilogy by Teri Woods. Many street-lit novels' plots are centered on the romantic adventures and entanglements of young couples. Romance readers would enjoy thug fiction, the subgenre spearheaded by author Wahida Clark.

Speculative: Some literary fiction within the speculative fiction genre is set in inner-city locations, like street lit. Some titles include Zetta Elliott's *A Wish after Midnight* (2010), where Genna is a teen girl living in inner-city Brooklyn. She travels back in time to pre–Civil War Brooklyn with a schoolmate. Nalo Hopkinson's *Brown Girl in the Ring* (1998) is about a single mother, Ti-Jeanne, who is trying to survive in a volatile futuristic city environment while reconciling her latent supernatural gifts. Octavia Butler's *Mind of My Mind* (1977) is about Mary, who was born and raised in the 'hood. Her telepathic powers are so powerful that she can attract the best and brightest telepaths to declare war on their leader, Doro.

Street lit is a blended genre that incorporates plot devices from various genres: romantic stories, mystery and speculative stories, and stories that approach fantasy and science fiction. Street lit features many trilogies and series that attract readers as they enjoy ongoing stories where the narrative and characters expand over time. Series can support readers' information literacy by providing motivation to read and see a story to completion, coming to an understanding of layered character and plot development spanning a period of time, learning to discern good storytelling, and employing successful reading strategies that merit a joy for reading.

Relativity

Q: Do you have to read something for a school assignment?

This question is essential for teen patrons who may have to read a novel for a school assignment. The librarian can still whet teens' appetite for street lit by referring them to established canonical texts such as

- *Oliver Twist* by Charles Dickens (1837–1839)
- *Maggie: A Girl of the Streets* by Stephen Crane (1893)
- *The Sport of the Gods* by Paul Laurence Dunbar (1902)
- *Native Son* by Richard Wright (1940)
- *The Street* by Ann Petry (1946)
- *Brown Girl, Brownstones* by Paule Marshall (1959)
- *Manchild in the Promised Land* by Claude Brown (1965)
- *The Autobiography of Malcolm X* by Malcolm X as told to Alex Haley (1965)
- *Down These Mean Streets* by Piri Thomas ([1967] 1997)
- *Bodega Dreams* by Ernesto Quiñonez (2000)

These titles are traditional literary works that feature street-lit themes such as the street as a performative stage, navigating poverty and other social issues, and coming of age through building relationships. When patrons come into the library asking for street lit, through the readers' advisory interview, it is possible to introduce them to classic and contemporary literature with street-lit elements. A successful readers' advisory interaction occurs when a patron leaves with more than they anticipated upon arrival at the library. With an open-minded, unbiased librarian, performing readers' advisory for street lit can promote information literacy and lifelong reading with teen and adult library patrons.

Authenticity

Q: Since you like realistic stories, what about nonfiction? How about authentic stories?

This is an essential question to consider because many believe street lit is just fiction, which is not true. The nonfiction side of the genre is prolific, with decades of documentation about the realities of living in inner-city neighborhoods. The nonfiction aspect of the genre combines the realism and storytelling of street fiction with the factual accuracy and research of nonfiction, coming in the form of autobiographies, memoirs, ethnographies, and research narratives.

Some nonfiction street-lit ethnographies and research narratives include

- *In Search of Respect: Selling Crack in El Barrio* by Phillippe Bourgois (1995)
- *The Corner: A Year in the Life of an Inner City Neighborhood* by David Simon and Edward Burns (1997)
- *Code of the Street: Decency, Violence and the Moral Life of the Inner City* by Elijah Anderson (1999)
- *Random Family: Love, Drugs, Trouble, and Coming of Age in the Bronx* by Adrian Nicole LeBlanc (2003)
- *We Beat the Street: How a Friendship Pact Led to Success* by Sampson Davis, George Jenkins, and Rameck Hunt, with Sharon M. Draper (2005)
- *Gang Leader for a Day: A Rogue Sociologist Takes to the Streets* by Sudhir Venkatesh (2008)
- *Reading Is My Window: Books and the Art of Reading in Women's Prisons* by Megan Sweeney (2010)
- *Between the World and Me* by Ta-Nehisi Coates (2015)
- *Terraformed: Young Black Lives in the Inner City* by Joy White (2020)

A wealth of *memoirs and biographies* also chronicle street-life experiences and illustrate the intensities of lower-income city living. Some titles include the following:

- *Monster: The Autobiography of an L. A. Gang Member* by Sanyika Shakur (1994)
- *Makes Me Wanna Holler: A Young Black Man in America* by Nathan McCall (1994)
- *Our America: Life and Death on the South Side of Chicago* by LeAlan Jones and Lloyd Newman with David Isay (1998)
- *Project Girl* by Janet McDonald (2000)
- *My Bloody Life: The Making of a Latin King* by Reymundo Sanchez (2000)

- *Living at the Edge of the World: A Teenager's Survival in the Tunnels of Grand Central Station* by Tina S. and Jamie Pastor Bolnick (2000)
- *Blue Rage, Black Redemption: A Memoir* by Stanley Tookie Williams (2004)
- *Grace after Midnight: A Memoir* by Felicia "Snoop" Pearson and David Ritz (2007)
- *Lady Q: The Rise and Fall of a Latin Queen* by Reymundo Sanchez and Sonia Rodriguez (2008)
- *The Beautiful Struggle* by Ta-Nehisi Coates (2008)
- *Buck: A Memoir* by M. K. Asante (2013)
- *Time: The Untold Story of the Love That Held Us Together When Incarceration Kept Us Apart* by Fox Richardson and Rob Richardson (2023)
- *Chronicles of the Juice Man: A Memoir* by Juicy J and Soren Baker (2023)

Urban stories conveyed as real-life narratives in biographies, memoirs, ethnographies, and research narratives can educate readers about urban culture and provide a platform for marginalized voices to be heard. Street literature as nonfiction can help readers raise their awareness about social issues such as poverty and societal injustice and gain insight into the nuances of urban culture. The power of reading street lit through a nonfiction lens is that stories based on real people's real lives can help readers understand the challenges and realities of urban life, as well as the resilience and hope of urban communities.

READERS' ADVISORY DISPLAY

Nonfiction titles could be coupled with similar fiction titles for an effective readers' advisory display. See Table 4.1 for an example. Librarians can also match street-lit novels with canonical works to foster teen readers' information literacy; see Table 4.2 for an example. Teens could read two novels to compare and heighten their critical thinking and analysis skills. See Table 4.3 for another idea for a readers' advisory display—matching street-lit titles with movies available in the library.

TABLE 4.1
Sample Coupling of Nonfiction and Fiction Titles for a Display

FICTION	NONFICTION
Monster by Walter Dean Myers (1999)	*Monster: The Autobiography of an L.A. Gang Member* by Sanyika Shakur (1994)
A Project Chick by Nikki Turner (2004)	*Project Girl* by Janet McDonald (2000)
The Coldest Winter Ever by Sister Souljah (1999)	*Random Family: Love, Drugs, Trouble, and Coming of Age in the Bronx* by Adrian Nicole LeBlanc (2003)
Ice by Will Robbins (2009)	*Blood Relation* by Eric Konigsberg (2005)
Sinful Vow: An Arranged Marriage Mafia Romance (Mafia Misfits) by Asia Monique (2022)	*Mafia Marriage: My Story* by Rosalie Bonanno with Beverly Donofrio (2003)
The Family Business by Carl Weber with Eric Pete, Treasure Hernandez, C. N. Phillips, and La Jill Hunt (2013–2023, 6-volume series)	*BMF: The Rise and Fall of Big Meech and the Black Mafia Family* by Mara Shalhoup (2010)

TABLE 4.2
Example of Matching Street-Lit Novels with Canonical Works

CONTEMPORARY	CANONICAL
The Coldest Winter Ever by Sister Souljah (1999)	*The Adventures of Moll Flanders* by Daniel Defoe (1722)
Wifey by Kiki Swinson (2004)	*Jane Eyre* by Charlotte Brontë (1847)
Keyshia and Clyde: A Novel by Treasure E. Blue (2008)	*The Sport of the Gods* by Paul Laurence Dunbar (1902)
Moth to a Flame by Ashley Antoinette (2010)	*Maggie: A Girl of the Streets* by Stephen Crane (1893)
Animal by K'wan Foye (2012)	*Invisible Man* by Ralph Ellison (1952)

TABLE 4.3

Example of Matching Books to Films

BOOK	FILM OR SERIES
True to the Game by Teri Woods (1994; 2007; 2008—trilogy)	*True to the Game* (2017; 2020; 2021)
Dutch by Kwame Teague and Teri Woods (2003; 2005; 2011—trilogy)	*American Gangster* (2007)
Black: A Street Tale by Tracy Brown (2003)	*Jason's Lyric* (1994)
The Cartel by Ashley and JaQuavis (2008–2023—10-volume series)	*Blow* (2001)
Shetani's Sister by Iceberg Slim (2015)	*Training Day* (2001)
Carl Weber's Kingpins: Philadelphia by Brittani Williams (2015)	*BMF: Starz Series* (2021; 2023)
Animal by K'wan Foye (2012–2017—five volumes)	*Luther: BBC Series* (2011–2013; 2015; 2019) + *Luther: The Fallen Sun* (2023)
Midnight by Sister Souljah (2008; 2011; 2016—trilogy)	*The Equalizer* (2014; 2018; 2023)
Kiss the Girls and Make Them Cry by Brittani Williams (2018)	*Hustlers* (2019)
Platinum Persuasion by India (2021)	*A Thousand and One* (2023)

Implications of Book Displays

Because the genre is essentially leisure reading, I suggest presenting street-lit readers' advisory displays for summer reading programs and Christmas holiday reading. Library displays during these times coincide with extended school and vacation breaks for students and working adults. A street-lit display for Black History Month would be inappropriate because such a display would insinuate that the genre is monolithic, appealing to just one population of people, which it is not and does not. Such a display also inaccurately situates the genre in a vacuum, as if the genre has no other history, which is untrue (see chapter 2).

A public library in Westchester, New York, effectively used book displays to highlight and elevate street-lit titles. Here, librarians separated the genre and created a display case that sat in front of the general fiction section. The case included featured titles merchandised to attract patron attention. Other titles were arranged in a tiered, flat formation to bring attention to the eye-catching cover designs. Staff also placed signage around the library, strategically positioned to highlight the collection.

I used a rolling book cart to house and promote the street-lit collection in my professional practice. The main benefit of this display was the portability of the collection. The rolling cart was useful for helping patrons at the checkout counter and in other areas of the library for readers' advisory. Another advantage of the rolling book display was when I had book club sessions for teen patrons: the cart made the genre readily available during book club meetings. Essential features of the "urban fiction cart" (as it was called back then) were the following:

- in-house-created genre labels for the books via a graphics editor
- signage to identify the collection from near and far
- checkout information posted right on the cart (e.g., no more than three books per patron at a time, with a maximum loan period of seven days)
- portability of the cart to different areas of the library (e.g., adult fiction, young adult fiction, circulation and checkout, reference desk, programs)

Implications for Library Circulation

The readers' advisory display is an excellent way to couple current street-lit fiction with classic, literary fiction, nonfiction, and audiovisual titles. Patrons learn how the genre is situated within the literary tradition and the library space. A multiformat readers' advisory display (along with shorter, quicker borrowing periods as indicated earlier) may even deter the high loss rate for street-lit novels because patrons can expand their view of the genre as it is connected to other books and materials. This might ignite an interest in patrons to try other titles and to return their books to the library to read other items on display, which in turn can positively affect circulation. This is not a guaranteed approach because patron communities respond to readers' advisory and outreach efforts differently. However, some materials displayed for street lit are a readers' advisory initiative worth the effort, time, and presentation. Finally, librarians should be aware of what is circulating and in demand for their library. Street lit is a well-read and requested genre. Librarians should provide access to requested and reviewed titles.

STREET-LIT BOOK REVIEW RESOURCES

Librarians and teachers, by and large, do not want to censor or block access to reading materials that patrons and students want to read. What often makes educators a barrier to reading materials is their need for more knowledge of credible book review resources for genres. For street lit, there are a few suitable venues for locating titles. NoveList is the premier database for finding book titles by author, title, genre, and appeal factors. Goodreads has a section called "Street Lit," where titles, relevant booklists, and online reading groups are displayed. For librarianship, traditional book review resources such as *Kirkus Reviews, Booklist,* and *Publishers Weekly* list new titles with reviews as they are published.

However, the patrons are the best resources for authors, titles, and trends. Patrons come off the street into the library to read about the street. They bring their experiences and word-of-mouth expertise about what titles are hot and who the quality authors are. Getting good information from patrons requires librarians to trust the patrons' insights and information. Librarians can follow up on that information to confirm and support title and author requests via professional book reviews from the resources cited here. In this social media age, information can be followed up and confirmed via search engine mining, book retailer website tagging (e.g., Amazon and Barnes & Noble), Facebook author and publisher pages, and Twitter lists and feeds.

THE LIBRARIAN'S STANCE ON READERS' ADVISORY

The librarian's stance on readers' advisory for street lit requires the librarian to be fully engaged as a culturally sensitive information gatherer, qualifier, and researcher. A culturally sensitive and competent approach to readers' advisory for street literature requires the librarian to research the genre, read the fiction and nonfiction, understand its availability in various formats, and situate the genre within literary tradition by making thematic connections between contemporary novels and literature of yesteryear. In this vein, the librarian then serves as an educator in presenting and promoting the best that street lit offers alongside established titles of similar stories and characters. Above all, the librarian must listen, respect, and positively respond to their patrons' expertise about what they want to read.

CHAPTER 5

Collection Management Considerations for Street Lit

To create a foundational street-lit collection, librarians ought to understand how the genre evolves and grows as new authors and titles are published. It is especially helpful to consider the significance of street lit's typical format and characteristics, study the classic titles that laid the foundation for the genre, and understand common collection development issues. "Street literature" is all-encompassing in its identity and includes formats like memoirs, poetry, and biographies. This chapter explores street-lit collection development, management, and promotion strategies to prolong the shelf life of a genre.

CIRCULATIONS TRENDS

The 1999 publication of *The Coldest Winter Ever* sparked prolific authorship and readership of street-lit fiction nationwide during the early 2000s. From 2000 to 2015, street-lit novels were voluminously checked out with a low rate of return. Circulation rates for major street-lit titles showed that libraries owned multiple copies, with a low number of these copies available on the shelves, compared to many copies being checked out, along with phantom copies that were "lost" or "missing." Table 5.1 illustrates that, while a library may own many copies, titles are often not readily available at library locations not only because they are lost or missing as a result of patron behavior but also because of library processing, cataloging, or because they are stuck in transit between library locations. Either way, the deeper meaning of table 5.1 is that, by and large, across the country, street lit, during its heyday of the early 2000s, was heavily owned by libraries but not necessarily consistently available. Public libraries often do not get full circulation (i.e., a book that is checked out is later checked back into the library) on street-lit novels because readers may borrow the books from the library and then pass them along to other readers; a typical pattern is for the books to get lost within a networked web of readers sharing one title.

TABLE 5.1

Circulation Cross-section of Large Public Libraries on August 3, 2010 (Paperback Format)

LIBRARY SYSTEM	*PUSH* BY SAPPHIRE (1996)	*THE COLDEST WINTER EVER* BY SISTER SOULJAH (1999)	*QUEEN BITCH* SERIES, PART 4 BY JOY DEJA KING (2008)
South—Durham (NC) County Library	45 copies 19 available 17 checked out 9 unavailable	29 copies 14 available 8 checked out 7 unavailable	0 copies
Northeast—Free Library of Philadelphia	205 copies 78 available 112 checked out 15 unavailable	82 copies 16 available 34 checked out 32 unavailable	13 copies 0 available 4 checked out 9 unavailable
West—Los Angeles Public Library	225 copies 169 available 142 checked out 11 unavailable	51 copies 32 available 15 checked out 4 unavailable	7 copies 0 available 1 checked out 6 unavailable
Midwest—Chicago Public Library	463 copies 177 available 142 checked out 144 unavailable	133 copies 16 available 54 checked out 63 unavailable	69 copies 11 available 42 checked out 16 unavailable

This trend is consistent throughout stabilizing the supply-and-demand flow of street lit in public libraries. The titles for table 5.1 were chosen based on *Essence* magazine's bestsellers booklist from October 2009 for the first edition of this book. Table 5.2 recaptures the same titles to illustrate the stasis that street lit attained as the genre became normalized with a stable readership, akin to the romance, mystery, and horror genres, where a dedicated readership keeps the demand at a steady flow.

TABLE 5.2

Circulation Cross-section of Large Public Libraries on July 11, 2023 (Paperback Format)

LIBRARY SYSTEM	*PUSH* BY SAPPHIRE (1996)	*THE COLDEST WINTER EVER* BY SISTER SOULJAH (1999)	*QUEEN BITCH* SERIES, PART 4 BY JOY DEJA KING (2008)
South—Durham (NC) County Library	3 copies 3 available 0 checked out 0 unavailable	5 copies 0 available 5 checked out 0 unavailable	2 copies 2 available 0 checked out 0 unavailable
Northeast—Free Library of Philadelphia	10 copies 7 available 0 checked out 3 unavailable	37 copies 11 available 6 checked out 20 unavailable	1 copy 1 available 0 checked out 0 unavailable
West—Los Angeles Public Library	25 copies 22 available 3 checked out 0 unavailable	104 copies 89 available 15 checked out 0 unavailable	0 copies
Midwest—Chicago Public Library	69 copies 58 available 11 checked out 0 unavailable	131 copies 24 available 49 checked out 58 unavailable	8 copies 6 available 0 checked out 2 unavailable

"Unavailable" status means the book is lost, missing, damaged, in cataloging, on hold, or otherwise unavailable for checkout. Overall, "unavailable" includes the number of checked-out copies added to the number of unavailable copies.

We also must consider that tables 5.1 and 5.2 give us a glimpse into the arc of street-lit readership over time, notwithstanding the multiple formats in which street-lit titles are now accessible. For example, the three titles sampled here—*Push, The Coldest Winter Ever,* and *Queen Bitch,* Part 4—are all available in e-book format from the library systems illustrated. *Push* is also available for loan as a movie titled *Precious: Based on the Novel Push by Sapphire,* released in 2009 in theaters nationwide. Even though the number of copies of *The Coldest Winter Ever* has stabilized from its popularity during the earlier 2000s, the drop in number of copies may also be due to a distribution of copies purchased across formats and the purchase of the *Midnight* trilogy (2008; 2011; 2016) that Sister Souljah published as part of *The Coldest Winter Ever* series.

Purchasing street-lit titles should be based on a sustainable model where the classics or must-haves of the genre (see appendix) are maintained alongside a cyclical selection of in-demand titles based on publication status (e.g., on the *New York Times* Best Sellers list, reputable book reviews, an established author with a new release) and reader interest in your community. Book reviews from traditional resources are encouraged, but they also may not feature this genre. Online reader reviews are an essential consideration when researching new titles. Reader reviews from Amazon.com and Goodreads are the most current and well-regarded at the time of the writing of this book. Lastly, NoveList is very helpful in distinguishing YA street lit from adult street lit so that the community has equitable access to appropriate materials that meet readers' interests and information needs. The subject heading "urban fiction" can be applied when searching databases like NoveList or WorldCat to locate titles. It is vital to pay attention to the multiple formats that street lit comes in: print, graphic novels, e-books, audiobooks, and film.

SEXUAL CONTENT, THE LIBRARIAN, AND CENSORSHIP

Another issue with developing a street-lit collection is the genre's racy content and determining how appropriate the genre can be for a library's collection with a given readership, particularly for YA readers instead of adult readers. Some titles are more sexually and violently explicit than others (this is also true for the romance, thriller, and horror genres) and may not be appropriate for more conservative communities and readers. Although it is not to be confused with urban erotica, street lit's sexual explicitness often prompts librarians to ban and censor the genre. In formal and informal interviews with urban and suburban public librarians, librarians have been known not to select or purchase street lit, or, if it is purchased by central processing, not to process street lit for addition to library shelves, to hide street-lit novels (print and graphic novel formats) in reference desk drawers, or to merchandise street lit in locked display cases (Irvin, 2012; Boyd, 2018).

A diplomatic approach to balance this censorship issue is for librarians first to consider titles recommended from established professional and scholarly resources (i.e., book review lists, professional columns, and articles in print and on the web). Thus, if any challenges arise for a street-lit title, the librarian has professional justification via documentation and scholarship to support the material. Field research shows many teachers and librarians admitting to confiscating (teachers) or censoring (librarians) street-lit books. School media specialist and scholar K. C. Boyd warns of librarian bias that can lead to censoring or banning street-lit books because the "students can really benefit from these cautionary tales" (Boyd, 2018).

The most important consideration when developing a street-lit collection is that the cream rises to the top, with librarians providing the best genre representation. As in any other literary genre, street lit has its classics, must-haves, and shelf sitters. Librarians can discern which is which by becoming active readers and employing professional protocols for determining appropriate titles.

SUBGENRES AND COLLECTION DEVELOPMENT

There are classic titles that are requisite for any reputable collection, and then there are criteria to consider when choosing must-haves for a well-rounded collection. Classic titles of street lit are classic because they set the bar for the prolific nature of the genre, have stood the test of time in terms of reader interest and demand, and have remained standard-bearers for readership since their publication. Street lit is also known for its prolific series titles—many stories are published with cliff-hangers, promising sequels, trilogies, and entire multivolume series. Some titles are trilogies, whereas some series are beyond six-volume installments and can virtually claim their library shelf.

Street-Lit Classics

The following list of titles presents a foundational collection for street lit. These titles have stood the test of time for reader interest, collection development, and publication accessibility (i.e., they continue to be in print).

- *The Coldest Winter Ever*—Sister Souljah (1999) and *Life After Death: The Coldest Winter Ever,* Part 2 (2021)
- *True to the Game*—Teri Woods (1994)
- *Flyy Girl*—Omar Tyree (1993)
- *B-More Careful*—Shannon Holmes (2000)
- *Let That Be the Reason*—Vickie M. Stringer (2009)
- *Black: A Street Tale*—Tracy Brown (2003)
- *Moth to a Flame*—Ashley Antoinette (2010)
- *The Cartel*—Ashley and JaQuavis (2008)
- *Bodega Dreams*—Ernesto Quiñonez (2000)
- *Push*—Relentless Aaron (2001)
- *Thugs and the Women Who Love Them*—Wahida Clark (2002)
- *Dutch*—Teri Woods and Kwame Teague (2003)
- *A Hustler's Wife*—Nikki Turner (2003)
- *Push*—Sapphire (1996)
- *Gangsta*—K'wan Foye (2003)
- *Animal*—K'wan Foye (2012)
- *The Family Business*—Carl Weber with Eric Pete (2013)
- *Wifey*—Kiki Swinson (2004)
- *Harlem Girl Lost: A Novel*—Treasure E. Blue (2004)
- *Bitch: The Beginning*—Joy Deja King (2010)

These titles are representative of the genre as a whole because, by and large, these authors have established themselves as writers and publishers of quality titles after a decade or more into the twenty-first-century era of this genre. (For a complete list of recommended street-lit titles, see the appendix.)

There are a few salient reasons why these titles and authors set the bar for street lit:

1. The titles all tell street tales that are candid, realistic, and uncompromising in characterizations and plot developments that exhibit a tension between characters and their relationship to their surroundings, thus contributing to the naturalist style of American literary tradition.

2. The realism of the stories makes an immediate impact on readers. That impact continues beyond the book to focus on the author himself or herself and the author's subsequent contributions to the genre (e.g., readers waited patiently for eight years for Sister Souljah's next book after *The Coldest Winter Ever*).

3. Most of the titles were the debut novels of their authors, yet affected the reading public such that many of the books became bestsellers (whether they were bestsellers on the street, particularly K'wan Foye and Teri Woods), via media outlets such as the *Essence* magazine and Urban Books bestsellers lists (i.e., *True to the Game, Let That Be the Reason, A Hustler's Wife*), or via the *New York Times* Best Sellers list (i.e., *The Coldest Winter Ever* and *Flyy Girl*). Furthermore, most of the authors on this canonical list started in the genre as entrepreneurs, independently selling their books on the street.

Teri Woods is credited with spearheading the entrepreneurial aspect of street lit, which was the backbone of the genre's success as a literary force during the early 2000s. During the late 1990s, Woods peddled her books on 125th Street in New York City, selling over one hundred thousand copies. Author Relentless Aaron also sold over one hundred thousand copies of his books before signing with a mainstream publisher, St. Martin's Press. With the pervasiveness of the internet, authors have moved online to market their books. The paperback is still a popular format in libraries, but for nonlibrary readers, the e-book is a popular format for accessing street lit. On Amazon.com, street-lit novels are regularly published straight to e-book format, where readers can purchase novels for as low as ninety-nine cents on Kindle. E-books are popular, as they are easy to download and read on various devices, and readers can readily engage in book discussions via reviewer feedback on platforms such as Amazon and Goodreads.

Street-Lit Fiction Series

Street fiction boasts many highly regarded series that must be included in a solid urban fiction collection. Case in point, most of the titles in table 4.3 are the first installments in trilogies or series. In addition to *The Coldest Winter Ever* and *Life after Death* (*The Coldest Winter Ever,* Part 2), Sister Souljah published the *Midnight* trilogy (2008; 2011; 2016), which features one of the characters from *The Coldest Winter Ever*, Midnight, as the protagonist. In 2014, Souljah also published *A Deeper Love Inside: The Porsche Santiaga Story* (2014), a prequel to *The Coldest Winter Ever*, told in the voice of Winter Santiaga's younger sister. Other classic titles that were the first installments of trilogies include Teri Woods's *True to the Game*, Dutch titles, and Nikki Turner's *Hustler's Wife*.

Street lit is prolific with series. From table 4.3, K'wan's *Animal* is the beginning of a five-volume series, and Wahida Clark's *Thugs and the Women Who Love Them* sparked a seven-volume series known as the *Thug* series. Ashley and JaQuavis's *The Cartel* begins a ten-volume series that ends with the two titles *Long Live the Cartel* (2020) and *Cartel Queen: Aries Manifesto* (2023).

Additionally, Deja King's *Bitch* series (with eleven installments) has maintained its popularity with its closing title, *Bitch The Final Chapter*, holding a 4.7 reader rating on Amazon and Goodreads. However, some communities may balk at the series' title. Thus, aside from King's series, other well-read trilogies and series include but are not limited to *Around the Way Girls* (twelve volumes), *Girls from the Hood* (fourteen books), and Carl Weber's *Kingpins* series, which boasts fifteen volumes.

Investing in purchasing these series can contribute to a circulating street-fiction collection in virtually any public library responsive to the street-lit readership community. The series is valuable for developing a street-fiction collection because the varied stories provide a pluralistic view of the genre and the inner-city culture it illustrates. The power of the serialization of street fiction is demonstrated through a collection of stories that cover varied regions of the United States, the Caribbean, and beyond, thus representing various languages, dialects, and locations to provide a healthy mix of women's and men's stories, as well as multicultural stories (e.g., Latino, African American, LGBTQ), offering a stable representation of established authors who have a significant readership and fan base. Thus, many readers know about these titles or authors, and the known authors, creative titles, and relatable book covers attract readers to the collection.

ATTRIBUTES OF REPUTABLE STREET-FICTION COLLECTIONS

In addition to the classics and series titles, a well-rounded street-fiction collection would include titles that invariably feature the following attributes:

- Written in Standard American English (SAE), with authentic language (African American, Latino, or regional dialect, lingo, and slang interwoven in the dialogue—SAE is a sanctioned academic assignation for Standard American English, as is AAVE for African American Vernacular English).
- Authored by established writers who have published consistently reputable titles in the genre, including but not limited to:
  - Relentless Aaron
  - Mark Anthony
  - Treasure E. Blue
  - Chunichi
  - Wahida Clark
  - Ashley and JaQuavis Coleman
  - K. Elliott

- K'wan Foye
- Erick S. Gray
- E. L. Griffin
- Treasure Hernandez
- Blake Karrington
- Joy Deja King
- C. N. Phillips
- Sister Souljah
- Vickie M. Stringer
- T. Style
- Nikki Turner
- Carl Weber
- Anthony Whyte
- Teri Woods

- Authored by up-and-coming, must-read authors who may be referred by patrons, colleagues, book review resources, and street book vendors.
- Packaged preferably in slightly oversized paperback or e-book format with a colorful, attractive cover and catchy title, usually indicative of street lingo (e.g., *Diary of a Street Diva*, *Street Dreams*, *Gunmetal Black*).
- Published by established publishing outlets, including, but not limited to, the following:

  - Dafina, an imprint of Kensington Publishing
  - Grand Central Publishing
  - Simon & Schuster
  - St. Martin's Griffin
  - Urban Books

- Reviewed by credible review sources such as

  - Amazon
  - Barnes & Noble
  - *Book Review Digest*
  - *Kirkus Reviews*
  - *Library Journal*
  - *New York Times*
  - *Publishers Weekly*

- *School Library Journal*
- Urban Reviews Online

Street lit has a robust entrepreneurial bent that the library world must respect. Patrons often come into the library suggesting or asking for titles they saw on street-vendor tables in the neighborhood. It is vital to locate relevant titles that may need to be readily available via nontraditional book vendors. Also, e-book reader reviews on platforms like NoveList, Amazon.com, and Goodreads should be explored.

STREET-LIT NONFICTION

Many titles in the nonfiction collection depict the real-life survival stories of American city dwellers. These books are biographies, memoirs, poetry, and some research materials. Notably, considerable socio-anthropological and ethnographic research works that tell the stories of citizens surviving street life in various ways have been published. Some classic titles include (in order of publication)

Biographies or Memoirs

Makes Me Wanna Holler by Nathan McCall (1994)

My Bloody Life: The Making of a Latin King by Reymundo Sanchez (2000)

Project Girl by Janet McDonald (2000)

Living at the Edge of the World: A Teenager's Survival in the Tunnels of Grand Central Station by Tina S. and Jamie Pastor Bolnick (2000)

E.A.R.L.: The Autobiography of DMX by DMX as told to Smokey D. Fontaine (2003)

I Choose to Stay: A Black Teacher Refuses to Desert the Inner City by Salome Thomas-El with Cecil Murphey (2004)

From Pieces to Weight: Once Upon a Time in Southside Queens by 50 Cent with Kris Ex (2005)

Grace after Midnight: A Memoir by Felicia "Snoop" Pearson and David Ritz (2007)

War of the Bloods in My Veins: A Street Soldier's March toward Redemption by DeShaun "Jiwe" Morris (2008)

A Question of Freedom: A Memoir of Learning, Survival, and Coming of Age in Prison by R. Dwayne Betts (2009)

Fist Stick Knife Gun: A Personal History of Violence by Geoffrey Canada, Adapted by Jamar Nicholas (2010)—graphic novel based on the original 1995 memoir by Canada

The Other Wes Moore: One Name, Two Fates by Wes Moore (2010)

Buck: A Memoir by M. K. Asante (2013)

Socio-anthropological Ethnographies (Documentary Research)

Crackhouse: Notes from the End of the Line by Terry Williams (1992)

In Search of Respect: Selling Crack in El Barrio by Phillippe Bourgois (1995)

Rosa Lee: A Mother and Her Family in Urban America by Leon Dash (1997)

Our America: Life and Death on the South Side of Chicago by LeAlan Jones and Lloyd Newman with David Isay (1998)

Code of the Street: Decency, Violence, and the Moral Life of the Inner City by Elijah Anderson (1999)

Random Family: Love, Drugs, Trouble, and Coming of Age in the Bronx by Adrian Nicole LeBlanc (2003)

Gang Leader for a Day: A Rogue Sociologist Takes to the Streets by Sudhir Venkatesh (2008)

Lady Q: The Rise and Fall of a Latin Queen by Reymundo Sanchez and Sonia Rodriguez (2008)

Righteous Dopefiend by Phillippe Bourgois (2009)

Grand Central Winter: Stories from the Street by Lee Stringer (2010)

The South Side: A Portrait of Chicago and American Segregation by Natalie Y. Moore (2016)

Three Girls from Bronzeville: A Uniquely American Memoir of Race, Fate, and Sisterhood by Dawn Turner (2021)

Poetry

Close to Death: Poems by Patricia Smith (1993)
The Rose That Grew from Concrete by Tupac Shakur (1999)
Speak the Unspeakable by Jessica Holter (2000)
Bum Rush the Page: A Def Poetry Slam edited by Tony Medina and Louis Reyes Rivera, foreword by Sonia Sanchez (2001)
The Moments, the Minutes, the Hours: The Poetry of Jill Scott by Jill Scott (2005)
The Dead Emcee Scrolls: The Lost Teachings of Hip-Hop by Saul Williams (2006)
Street Love by Walter Dean Myers (2006)
Please by Jericho Brown (2008)

NONFICTION AND FICTION ALONG THE HISTORICAL CONTINUUM

The publication years for nonfiction street-lit titles parallel the renaissance period for fiction street-lit titles, circa 1999 to the present day. It is important to note that while authors began to tell their stories via fiction, researchers and literary writers were also publishing the same kinds of nonfiction stories at the same time. This parallel time line connects to the historical and literary continuum of the emergence of the naturalist literary movement at the turn of the nineteenth century into the twentieth century (1880s–1940s).

Authors like Stephen Crane, Mario Puzo, and Abraham Cahan published street-lit novels depicting the realistic, raw, and gritty tales of Irish, Italian, and Jewish immigrants living in inner-city enclaves at the turn of the twentieth century. Richard Wright, Ann Petry, and Chester Himes extended the naturalist literary movement into African American literary tradition with their street-lit stories depicting the harsh realities of American Blacks' uneasy adjustment to city life during the Great Northern Migration (circa 1910–1970)—notably, Paul Laurence Dunbar's *The Sport of the Gods* (1902) was an early contribution to the naturalist movement within African American literary tradition.

During the Civil Rights Era, street-lit fiction and nonfiction classics such as Claude Brown's novel *Manchild in the Promised Land* (1965) and Malcolm X's autobiography, *The Autobiography of Malcolm X* (1965), continued the realism and naturalism strain in the storytelling of the inner-city Black experience. Donald Goines and Iceberg Slim carried the style with their raw, pulp-fiction street-lit novels of the 1970s. At the turn of the twenty-first century, we have American Black and Hispanic or Latino American authors like Sister Souljah and Jeff Rivera alongside Reymundo Sanchez and Jessica Holter telling their tales of daily living in inner-city enclaves from both sides of the aisle, fiction and nonfiction, just as in yesteryear, with novelists being published at the same time that street literature in the form of broadsides, pamphlets, and chapbooks were circulating and being sold on the streets (Shepard, 1973). The streets always have stories to tell, authentic stories about the people who live in urban ghettos. Rapper and actor Ice-T said it best in his foreword to Iceberg Slim's last published novel, *Doom Fox* (1998, ix): "Change the conditions of the ghetto, and the stories will change." A Philadelphia teen street-lit book club member once said, "It's all real. Fiction, nonfiction. It's all the same. It's life. It's all real."

COLLECTION DEVELOPMENT STRATEGIES

The demand for street fiction can go beyond what libraries supply, especially when new titles are released and make the *New York Times* Best Sellers list. Many libraries contend with a high theft rate of street fiction. A few strategies can be employed to lower the theft rate and incentivize the return of the books for full circulation. Techniques include the following:

Allow a Maximum Number of Titles Per Patron (Suggested Maximum of Three)

Readers read the books quickly. When teens were asked how long it takes for them to read a street-lit novel, they reported: "sometimes a day," and "less than a week" (Morris et al., 2006). Because of this, instead of one patron checking out a stack of six to a dozen titles at one time, allow patrons to check out just three titles that they must return on a seven-day loan.

Circulate Street-Lit Collections on a Seven-Day Loan

Readers read the books quickly, and if they have another two weeks (or longer) to return the books, it is during this window of time that they may loan the book to another reader and then another, and ultimately, the book is lost in a web of readers—degrees of separation away from the original borrower of the book. If readers read the text within the first week of checking it out of the library, they are more likely to remember that the book is due at the library and it will be returned on time.

Interfile—Mix It Up

Interfile street fiction with the rest of the fiction collection to heighten patrons' exposure to more of the library's fiction collection; this also lets readers know that street fiction does not sit outside or beyond other literary fiction works. Keep street fiction within literary tradition on the shelves.

If there is high demand for the genre, a cluster collection could be arranged at the beginning of the fiction collection, especially if your fiction collection is arranged by genre. Highlight the street-fiction collection alongside romance or mystery so that patrons experience browsing through the street lit as a part of a broader range of materials.

Combine fiction and nonfiction titles as a cluster collection. This tactic could be a good book display for summer reading, Christmas vacation reading, spring break reading, and to promote author events. A combined fiction and nonfiction collection shows that the genre is to be taken seriously, as fiction and nonfiction often depict similar reality-based narratives.

Make the Cluster Collection Portable

A public librarian from New York reported situating a small cluster collection of street lit alongside the computer sign-up station in the library because that is where patrons focused their energies while in the library. This approach heightened exposure to the materials and consequently increased checkout of books.

Another librarian working as a branch manager in Los Angeles described creating a cluster collection on a small book cart so patrons could take the cart where they sat in the library to browse the collection. This approach invariably increased the number of books the patron wanted to check out. This strategy also increased readers' advisory interactions between patron and librarian.

Another school librarian from Minneapolis stationed a small "What's Hot!" collection on her desk to track what was being checked out, what needed to be shelved, and what needed to be reordered.

One public librarian from Philadelphia kept multiple copies of classic street-fiction titles specifically as an outreach collection she took with her and booktalked when visiting local high schools. When she got down to one copy of a title, that copy became "reference" (i.e., noncirculating) within the traveling outreach collection. She then booktalked the reference copy to encourage students to come to the library to get a circulating copy on library shelves. Having classic titles provided students with titles and authors they already knew; thus, they were empowered and engaged in the booktalk as experts of the genre. This exchange opened up space for the students to give suggestions to the librarian of hot, new titles and authors that she could add to her street-lit collection. Students invariably visited the library after a school visit to browse the in-house circulating collection because they felt confident entering and browsing the library after the readers' advisory interaction at school.

Combine the Old with the New

Put a "classic" label on what I like to call the big three of street lit: *The Coldest Winter Ever, Flyy Girl*, and *True to the Game*, and shelve them in your classics collection alongside John Steinbeck and Mary Shelley, Mark Twain and Leo Tolstoy, Alice Walker, and Richard Wright.

Put a "street lit" label on important street-literature works such as *The Autobiography of Malcolm X* by Malcolm X as told to Alex Haley, *The Street* by Ann Petry, and *The Real Cool Killers* by Chester Himes, and shelve them alongside KaShamba Williams and Relentless Aaron, Kiki Swinson and Chunichi, Shannon Holmes and K'wan Foye.

Listen to Patrons

Readers will share what new titles are coming out or which titles may be missing from an author or series. They may share the names of titles by entrepreneurial authors who may be accessible for adding to the library's collection. For example, during my time at the reference desk, it was patrons who introduced me to *The Coldest Winter Ever, Push, True to the Game, Flyy Girl*, and *B-More Careful* during the late 1990s when the street-lit renaissance began to take form. Patrons also told me about the Kiki Swinson *Wifey* series, and the same teen patrons told me to stop reading *Wifey* and check out *Jane Eyre*—yes, that *Jane Eyre*.

STRATEGY RESULTS

The librarians from across the US who employed the above strategies reported the following outcomes:

- *Interfiling street lit* increased the shelf life of a circulating street-lit collection by ten weeks.
- *A portable cluster collection* exposed readers to a broader range of literary works that fit into the same genre.

- *Combining canonical street literature with contemporary titles* increased readers' advisory conversations that have been educational for both the patron and the librarian.
- *Listening to patrons and building rapport with them* aided the positive return rate of borrowed materials back into the collection.

Of course, these strategies are not etched in stone. Try one or combine one with another, incorporating all strategies with an active discourse with your patrons, doing what is best for your community. Some of these methods may seem unconventional in their approach and application; however, they have been executed successfully in American public libraries in inner-city neighborhoods without any challenges from the community or other stakeholders. These strategies emphasize our educative mission and goals as public education servants while enhancing our abilities to do just that—serve.

CHAPTER 6

Library Programming for Street Lit

Library programming centered around the promotion and visibility of the street-lit genre can help engage reluctant readers, spark conversation within the community, and provide an opportunity to highlight, educate, and celebrate the genre's history and importance. Many creative strategies can be applied to marketing and programming for street lit. Book displays, book clubs, field trips, and literacy events provide valuable opportunities for patrons to engage with and learn about the genre.

It is essential to plan programming around street lit to support reading and learning for reluctant readers who may find entry into reading the genre because its writing style often represents everyday, relatable language, dialect, and slang. By promoting the genre's literariness across literary categories and formats by connecting fiction with nonfiction, books with DVDs, poetry with music, and canonical texts with contemporary texts, the library makes a statement that supports equitable access to texts that may serve as cultural artifacts. Engaging library patrons in reading circles or book clubs that read street lit helps educate readers about one another's ideas in response to reading various stories with various representations.

BOOK DISPLAYS

Book displays can be a very effective programming strategy in which the genre intersects with multiple literary formats. By setting up a book display that features titles of various reading levels and forms, readers from diverse perspectives may be attracted to the display, resulting in increased browsing of the library collection and heightened circulation of library materials.

For outreach purposes, street-lit titles can be displayed as part of a booktalking repertoire for the librarian. You are almost guaranteed rapt attention when you booktalk street-lit novels to city teens, particularly when you couple book titles with music titles. Librarians can also combine texts from other genres and movie titles to create a book display rich in coverage and depth. (See pairings in chapter 4.) If patrons like a particular book, they might enjoy a specific song; see table 6.1 for a sample of street lit and music pairings.

TABLE 6.1
Street Lit and Music Pairings

TITLE AND AUTHOR	SONG AND ARTIST
Road Dawgz by K'wan	"Ruff Ryders' Anthem" by DMX
True to the Game by Teri Woods	"Otherside of the Game" by Erykah Badu
Stackin' Paper by Joy King	"For the Money" by Fabolous and Nicki Minaj
The Cartel by Ashley and JaQuavis	"How I Got Over" by The Roots

BOOK CLUBS

Forming a book club around this genre is probably the most effective way to engage library patrons in reading street lit and embracing the reading habit as a vital part of one's lifelong learning modus operandi. The genre seems to excite and motivate readers to talk about what they read and why they read street lit (Sweeney,

2010). A browsing of street-lit titles on Amazon.com affirms that readers are experts in this genre. Reader comments on popular titles on Amazon.com often generate further reader response that is often rich in critical analysis. Many reader comments on the street-lit pages of Amazon.com exhibit a vast reading repertoire (Brooks and Savage, 2009).

Because of the prolific publishing nature of the genre, readers often want to read and discuss multiple titles during book club meetings. With teenagers, the developmental needs of self-definition and meaningful participation bolster their internal assets of commitment to learning and positive values when they can choose their titles to read and then actively discuss those titles in a book club setting (Alessio, 2004; Gorman and Suellentrop, 2009). Teens feel ownership and responsibility for the discourse of the book club. This stance aids in their emerging life skills of self-sufficiency and personal responsibility. Although multiple titles may sound confusing for a book club discussion, it is a requested approach for teen and adult readers. It empowers readers when they choose what to read rather than being prescribed one particular title based on a librarian's or teacher's expertise. Because readers often have experiential entry into the genre's stories, they are immediate experts on the genre's content and context. Thus, reader-driven title selection for the group is an essential strategy for a successful book club. Although a multiple-title approach allows for exposure and discussion of more books within the genre, a downside to the method is that readers may feel they are missing full engagement in a story they have not read. It is best, however, for book club members (teens and adults alike) to take ownership of the group structure and agenda so that opportunities for critically understanding what works and what does not work in a reading group become fodder for establishing a unique, workable identity for that group.

BOOK DISCUSSIONS AND ACTIVITIES

Book club discourse gives library patrons space to discuss street-lit stories critically. Book club meetings facilitated by a librarian or other educator allow readers to unpack various representations in the stories, pull up characterizations, plots, and themes, and problematize them to deepen personal understandings about community, personal identity, and how one can further construct one's identity.

Working with teen library patrons who read street lit is vital because their engagement with a reading community that is discussing literature critically further opens up opportunities for more literacy activities such as the collective authorship.

One positive outcome of teen book clubs reading street lit is that teens have been known to move from talking about street lit to collaboratively writing street lit. In one teen book club in Philadelphia, members worked up character outlines for protagonists and antagonists and devised a chapter-by-chapter outline each book club member took on and wrote themselves. The plot outline totaled nine chapters. Teens often engage in collaborative group work that evidences college-level reading and writing practices.

Writing Poetry and Journaling

Success has been observed with teen girls and boys using poetry and self-reflective journaling as a parallel exploration of street lit. Teens use book club meetings to bring poems they like, read poems from street-lit novels (e.g., *True to the Game*, *Black*, and *Upstate*), and share poetry they wrote during the book club and from their social media posts.

Self-Esteem Activities

Self-esteem activities invariably engaged teen girls, who would talk about street-lit stories and then question their self-esteem against female characters in the books. Girls would consider, "Is this me?" or challenge the character: "Why did she do that? Why did she put up with that?" This critical inquiry resulted in craft activities where teen girls wrote affirmations on heart-shaped cutouts, created collages from magazines, or reaffirmed one another through group talk, during which they would give one another advice and support about their personal lives.

These outcomes illustrate how engagement in a genre often considered controversial or lowbrow can garner multimodal literary and literacy-related results. Through various book club activities, we learn that urban teens are engaged in multiple literacy activities that are print-based as well as online. Of course, these strategies can also work successfully with adult book club groups.

Overall, the most critical thing a librarian can do in a street-lit book club is to listen to the readers. For many teens, the library is one of a few places where they can speak their minds about themselves and their daily issues. The library street-lit book club can be an essential platform where urban readers, specifically, can say how they relate to the stories (or not) in ways they need to say it; they also learn to listen to others as peers seek to be voiced and heard.

The teen library book club, when focusing on the genre of street lit, can be a forum for processing fictional and lived stories so that teens make meaning from living in communities that can be fast-paced and have an unorganized atmosphere. The street-lit book club is where daily living can be slowed down and reflected on in slow motion, allowing the sense to be made out of nonsensical neighborhood happenings. Teens can validate their questions, insights, and fears while reconciling them for heightened self-understanding and determination.

Case in point—with the teens I worked with when I began the book club, most book clubbers were in the sixth and seventh grades (circa 2005), with one or two attending high school. All the middle schoolers are grown up and attending college or post-secondary trade school six years later. Some older teens enlisted in the military with military tours in Iraq and Afghanistan. Some former library teens are parents now, working and living productive lives. The point here is that no one is in jail; no one is a prostitute or wifey, drug dealer or pimp, from reading street lit or from being in a book club focused on reading street lit. Today's teen reader is also literate on social media. When putting together book club engagement alongside social media engagement, it is clear that teens who read street lit are thinkers, readers, and writers. Their involvement with their neighborhood library, library staff, and library activities, such as the street-lit book club, contributes to their practices as lifelong readers.

BOOK CLUBS FOR LIBRARIANS

Library book club activities can help adults focus on self-reflection and inquiry for personal and professional development. Like any other genre, street lit can be used for reading group work and professional development for librarians, teachers, and other community-based educators. When reading what the patrons read, librarians learn of new authors, titles, songs, and platforms that inspire readers to visit the library to look for reading material. In a librarian book club, various formats of library materials that feature stories about inner-city living can be explored on all reading levels. For example, picture books such as Ezra Jack Keats's *A Snowy Day* (1962) and *Goggles!* (1969) can be informative for children's librarians, and graphic novels such as Donald Goines's *Daddy Cool* (1974), which was reissued as a graphic novel, and Eminem's biographical installment *In My Skin* (2004) can be helpful to young adult librarians.

Book club librarians learned strategies for readers' advisory for street lit (and genres across the board, for that matter) and for confronting ethical biases they did not realize they were carrying toward patrons, the literature, and various professional practices, such as collection development and management. Various practitioner inquiry activities were introduced and employed (and were also successfully executed with the teen book clubbers):

Reaction Sheets

After intense book club discussions, librarians wrote an anonymous paragraph recording their response to that session. The facilitator then collected the sheets. At the next book club meeting, the meeting opened up with the facilitator reading the responses. The responses then garnered further discussion. Reaction sheets were handy for approaching hard-to-discuss topics.

Polling

Consider creating polls for the group to ask questions about the readings and gain insight into discussion topics. For example, "How many of us have met Winter Santiaga [the protagonist of *The Coldest Winter Ever*] in the library? What was her information need? How did you meet that need?" These kinds of prompts encourage inquiry-based critical thinking for readers to engage in meaningful conversation about their reading responses to the literature.

Word Associations

When prevalent themes take up much of the discussion's focus, we would do a word association around a word or short phrase. Librarians would write down whatever words or phrases came to mind that they associated with the assigned meme. This stream-of-consciousness listing would last about one or two minutes. After the time was up, we shared our associations in a round-robin fashion, which manifested matching ideas, new ideas, and opposing ideas. This outcome would further discuss personal beliefs and how they signify professional practice.

Check-In

At the beginning or the end of the book club session, the facilitator would ask the group what is happening in their libraries: What is popular in your library right now? Who is checking out what? What are patrons saying about the collection? What do you think of that? Such questions allow participants to discuss and share professional experiences and best practices. This approach encourages librarians to engage in researching their own practice for the purpose of professional development.

These methods are strategies for practitioner inquiry; invariably, these various group reflection activities discuss professional practice (Cochran-Smith and Lytle, 2009). The very act of talking about the story, characters, and setting was enough for librarians to begin talking about their social interactions with patrons via readers' advisory and reference interviews. Most book club librarians report that practitioner inquiry helped them perceive their ideas and understandings about their service community, definitions of reading, assumptions about street literature and its readers, and their overall stance toward their professional identity as librarians. Street literature was a catalyst for reflective professional development.

Many exercises and activities can be introduced to dig deeper into a book discussion to pull connections from the stories to contemplate personal and professional reading, writing, and literacy practices. Librarians (and other educators) filling the role of book club facilitators must provide a confidential space for discourse for teen and adult readers of street lit. Because of various themes in the genre, such as violence, death, and sex, various questions, connections, and experiences may be shared that require the concealment of confidentiality. This approach does not mean that librarians and libraries become secret service counselors and agencies; it just means that everyone in the group respects one another's stories as sacred in the reading circle. This assurance is a foundation for authentic, open conversation and reflection about a genre that demands being heard.

FIELD TRIPS

Author book signings and lectures are excellent field trips for street-lit book clubbers. Many street-lit authors like K'wan, Vickie M. Stringer, Teri Woods, and T. N. Baker visit schools, libraries, and other local outlets to meet readers and promote their books. As a field trip, a book club can visit a bookstore or another literary location hosting an author event. Movies are another type of field trip for a street-lit book club. Book festivals and fairs are other important venues where street-lit authors and panel discussions are featured. For example, the Harlem Book Fair in New York and the Philadelphia Free Library Book Festival feature authors and topics related to the street-literature genre.

Field Trip Ideas for Street-Lit Readers
- author book signings and events
- street lit in cinema
- book club meetings at a café instead of the library
- local university free lectures or events
- book fairs, festivals, and expos
- literacy outreach events, such as
  - teens engaging in story time at a daycare center
  - public and school librarians collaborating on an author visit
  - teens distributing library program flyers at school
- cross-branch visits: for multi-branch city library systems, you can network with other librarians and have your book club visit their book club, and vice versa.

Field Trip Best Practices

The best approach for managing teens on field trips is to have them meet you at the venue, with confirmation of their parental/caregiver approval via signed permission slips (following your library's policies). Urban teens are adept at independently navigating mass transportation in the city. Field trips to public events with teens are successful when the teacher or librarian consistently promotes the event and incentivizes attendance with a door prize, or an award presented at the next book club meeting. The teens must understand that the event is free admission, and their attendance is their responsibility. Flyers can be posted in the library and given to teens to share with parents.

For the teen book club I facilitated, I promoted a street-lit author panel where I was the moderator for the Free Library of Philadelphia event. I invited the book clubbers to the event, reminding them that this was an opportunity to finally meet the authors they had been reading so they could ask questions. Six of the fifteen book clubbers attended the event: they sat right up front and asked author Teri Woods (*True to the Game* trilogy) a question during the Q&A portion of the program. This interaction led to Woods meeting and talking with the teens after the event, further leading to her visiting the book club at their library a month later. During the visit, Woods reviewed the book club's collaboratively composed street-lit story outline and offered insightful feedback. This experience attests to how literary field trips can result in impactful outcomes.

PROMOTING STREET LIT = PROMOTING LITERACY

Small, rural, or suburban libraries may have a different demand for street lit than urban locales. Nevertheless, we do know that street lit is appealing to readers beyond urban locations and that every kind of reader is reading the genre. We know this to be true because quite a few street-lit titles have appeared on the *New York Times* Best Sellers list (e.g., *The Coldest Winter Ever, True to the Game, Thug Lovin'*, and *The Cartel 2*), which indicates that a broad spectrum of readers are buying and reading street lit. Case in point, Taylor Nix (2009, para. 3) of the Urban Book Source 2009 stated that "an appearance on the New York Times Best-Sellers List is proof that there is a place for America's inner-city tale that mirrors the realities and struggles of urban Black life on the street. [Street lit] is reaching audiences far beyond local community bookstores, exposing the masses to a new style of writing that has been overlooked and ignored by mainstream America until recently." This being said, it is a good idea for public library locations beyond the city to include a representation of street-lit titles on library shelves. This representation would be best based on appropriate age, reading levels (teen-friendly versus A/YA street lit), and patron interest.

We can see how library programming focused on or related to street lit may engage patrons to check out more books and participate in library activities. However, enough cannot be said for the librarian's presence as a promoter and supporter of street lit as an entry into the act of reading. Street lit can serve as a gateway to a broader reading regimen; I have worked with street kids whose first fully read book (from cover to cover) was a street-lit title. Their sense of accomplishment at successfully reading a book motivated them to read another book, then another book, then another. I am proud to share that those teens are now attending college as of this writing.

Once, I polled the teen book clubbers in the North Philadelphia library where I worked and later volunteered and asked them, "What books have you read in the past six months?" It was the Christmas season then, so they recalled titles read from the end of the previous school year (June) to the end of the calendar year (December). Of the fifteen teens (eleven girls and four boys) who were there that day, we filled the blackboard with more than different titles (not including multiple references to the *Harry Potter* series), spanning eight distinct genres: mystery, romance, science fiction, African American biographies, classics, fantasy, horror, and poetry.

As illustrated in this chapter, reading street lit can be a powerful means to introduce and immerse readers into an exploration of reading a broad range of text. It is a worthy approach to push or promote street lit because it has been shown to engage even the reluctant or nontraditional reader in other kinds of literacy activities, such as a more varied reading of literary genres, writing various forms of prose, and creative artistic self-expression. Reading street lit and talking about and around street lit can spawn an exploration of reading the self—the self as a reader, the self as a writer, the self as an artist, and the self as a literate being in multiple contexts. I do not know any educator who would find a problem with that.

—————— CHAPTER 7 ——————

Reading Street Lit as a Literacy Practice

Inside the library, the author, reader, and librarian are all in conversation with one another. Authors are the conduits through which library collections are built because they create the materials housed in libraries (e.g., books, movies, music), readers inquire and use the collection, and librarians maintain and promote it. Thus, looking at street lit within a library context, we must consider how authors, readers, and librarians read and respond to the genre and one another. This consideration is important to explore because it is through books that we interact with one another as readers to make sense of our worlds. As librarians, we must always be mindful of who we are when we do what we do and with whom we do it.

THE ACTIVE AUTHOR

Street-lit authors often come from the streets of which they write. "[Some] Street Lit authors are ex-convicts and recovering drug addicts who began writing while in prison and rehab centers. Their personal experience with the life and culture they describe adds realism to their gritty, raw stories" (Morris et al., 2006, p. 18). Street-lit authors also write stories based on what they have lived and witnessed as working-class residents of inner-city and rural communities. As in any other literary genre, some authors may have never personally experienced their stories but write them because they want stories that have long been swept under the rug to be told.

Because many street-lit authors are from the communities they write about, readers who are from a similar neighborhood have immediate entry into reading the novels because the language, tone, settings, and characters are recognizable and relatable. The novel is a sociocultural artifact between the author and reader that establishes an understanding that the story exists and that it will be told and heard. The author claims voicedness to the reading of their world and strengthens the author-reader relationship by writing a story, and the reader imagines living that story by reading it. Both intentions are iterative and interactive when the reader reads the book. Therefore, when the reader decides to go past the cover and the title, the choice alone to read the book's content implies that the reader trusts the author's intent. As each page is read, that trust is further invested so the reader can engage in the story.

Finding Consistency and Routine through Reading

Although this trust of authorial intent may not have been the impetus for street-lit authors to write, this trust is an implicit covenant for readers. In communities where it can be challenging to maintain faith in stability or consistency because of the precarious vibe of confusion, chaos, violation, or assault, trusting what one reads within the ignited hermeneutic imagination of the environment of a street-lit novel is pivotal for readers. Pointedly, for teens to read narratives that play out the dramas that they "read" in their everyday lives without having to suffer the repercussions, wounds, or consequences of those dramas serves as cautionary reconciliation of "Yes, this is life in the 'hood," and "Been there, done that, I don't have to go out like that" (meaning, "I don't have to end up like that" or "That doesn't have to be me") and can be life-saving. Just as young adult fiction helps teens make sense of the meaning of their worlds, street lit serves the same purpose for readers living in the same settings as the stories.

The Author-Reader Connection

The author writes the book to talk to the reader, and once the book is written, the author becomes a reader of the book. The reader listens to the author by reading the text: there is a dialogue here. Eileen Landay (2004) tells us that reading fiction and biographies engages dialogue within oneself (the author to him- or herself and the reader to him- or herself), between the reader and the author, and when text is shared between different readers. In all these realms, street lit is a powerful conduit for readers to find the authentic voice within an American culture that otherwise keeps them marginalized and silenced. Where there was possibly no previous relatable voice in mainstream literature for inner-city readers, readers and writers felt this void and cried, "No!" They found voices from their own streets to write and document their culture. *Never Go Home Again* author Shannon Holmes (2004, p. 3) explains:

> The experience and quality that I bring to my writing can't be bought, faked, or learned in school.
>
> [R]eaders know that I know what I know.
>
> . . . Through my novels, I invite the readers to journey with me into the streets. Come see what I've seen. . . . Let me show the gritty and grimy undercarriage of society. The side that some in the working class don't acknowledge or are unaware of.

Street lit is a gritty genre that gives an authentic voice to the author and reader, bridging lived reality with the reality of the mind and validating the truth of one's existence. Thus, street lit is necessary for readers exposed to the genre because it informs that they are expert readers of their own lived worlds and that they have a voice and place not just in living but also in assessing and critiquing their American reality.

Chapter 7

THE EXPERT READER

In turn, when we think about the themes in street-lit narratives, we see true-to-life stories about a day in the life in the 'hood, where people may be experiencing employment challenges, struggling to navigate the educational process, participating in livelihoods supported by an underground economy, emoting intense personal relationships, and too many times dying at the point of someone's gun. Additionally, name-brand labels, cars, and accessories are detailed in the stories to create a vivid picture of what characters are wearing, driving, and consuming as citizens of a capitalistic society. Amid the chaos of walking the streets, interacting in relationships, finding jobs, going to school, and experiencing various levels of violence, characters look very expensive. Aside from the materialistic bent, these same street-lit narratives offer stories about young people working hard to resist the lure of the streets, families facing challenges head-on and succeeding, and men and women loving, living, and learning life lessons in relationships. Whether fiction or nonfiction, street lit tells stories from a spectrum of human experiences.

Street lit illustrates how low-income Americans are in just as hot pursuit of the American dream as their wealthier fellow citizens who live just as chaotic and disorganized lifestyles in suburban and upper-class enclaves (e.g., the many reality TV shows that are popular on cable and streaming channels). Canonical literature (e.g., Crane's *Maggie: A Girl of the Streets*, Puzo's *The Godfather*, and Fitzgerald's *The Great Gatsby*) reminds us that daily living has nothing to do with how much money a person earns, the color of one's skin, or the ethnicity of one's culture; it has everything to do with ways in which we seek to identify with and qualify for the consumerist, capitalistic, hegemonic culture called the American dream. Street lit embraces this same distinction.

Gaining Perspective

When readers read such themes and plots repeatedly, book after book (which they do), such reading ignites their imagination to locate themselves in the context of the stories (Doyle, 2005; Morris et al., 2006). Dennis Sumara (1996) advises that when we read, we respond to the text based on the social and cultural context in which the reading occurs. How teens read street lit when they are seventh graders can be very different from how they read the genre as tenth graders. For example, at a library teen book club in Philadelphia (2005–2008), during their middle school years, book clubbers responded to the genre with comments like, "It teaches what not to do," "It's ghetto fabulous!" However, by the time they were high schoolers (thus older, thus having experienced and read more things), their responses were more intricate and included analysis from a wider lens. For example, during one book club meeting, when the members were asked if they had read Kiki Swinson's *Wifey* (2004), a book clubber named Sharon (pseudonym) waved her hand dismissively and said, "That interfered with my *Jane Eyre*."

This kind of reader response shows that no matter who they are, readers do not read in a vacuum; it is nearly impossible to do so. Thus, Sharon's response was based on an entire field of her knowledge and experience, which included the canonical text *Jane Eyre*. Sharon was not alone. In response to her statement, another book clubber, Deena (pseudonym), chimed in and exclaimed something like, "You read that? Gurl, that was good, wasn't it?" Sharon and Deena then began a side conversation about the exciting drama of *Jane Eyre*.

It may be easier to dismiss these sophisticated responses by musing, *"Nah, this is impossible—this is not true."* However, such holistic responses by teen readers align with reader-response theory, which posits that readers pull from a repertoire of life experiences and bring those expectations to the texts they choose to read (Iser, 1978; Sumara, 1996). Just by the act of reading in and of itself, an "indeterminacy filling" occurs when the imagination is invoked (Sumara, 1996, p. 31). The indeterminate gap between the imagination and lived reality is filled when we read text, creating heightened thinking by the reader because the reader, by virtue of reading, must synthesize what is being read with what is being lived. Thus, when inner-city citizens read street lit, their imaginations re-create the stories' worlds inside their minds, which, in turn, they synthesize with their lived reality (comparison and contrast of identities and situations between the book and the reader), thus filling the gap between the imagination and reality.

Literary scholar Wolfgang Iser (1978) calls this filled gap a new world, a virtual text, a heightened, unique sense of how one "fits" into one's own lived world. American psychologist Jerome Bruner (1986) states that this gap is a function of "making the familiar strange" (p. 13), "transcending the particular" (p. 159), and negotiating and constructing reality via narrative.

Active Reading, Self-Reflection, and Analysis

Within this indeterminate gap, the reader has space to evaluate, assess, and make meaning of what they read to add to what they already know and to learn and process what they do not know. It is this gap, during the act of reading, whether as an insider to the story or not, where the lifelong learner lies. Through reading, readers either learn more about themselves or learn more about humanity as a whole. Either way, the act of reading adds to the reader's repertoire as a human being living a human experience (Iser, 1978).

Just the pure act of reading street lit validates the reality of urban inner-city life for those living it. The stories connect the fantastical (the drama and trauma of ghetto life) with narratives that convey, "Yes, this exists; yes, this is real." This validation empowers the reader to be open to negotiating the reading of their worlds, with an entry into synthesis, analysis, and evaluation of their environment, the people in it, and their location and interaction within their lived world. In street lit, the streets signify their stories back to the people of the streets.

This reading stance is powerful stuff. Street lit can affect readers in ways that challenge their worldview. The pure act of reading ignites a revelatory connection between what was previously viewed (or read) as scary, confusing, or even as entertainment, to a critical lens of personal interpretation. Once this bridge has been made, readers' worldview broadens, and they then ask critical and nuanced questions like the following, from an Amazon.com post on *Thug Lovin'*, part 4, from June 26, 2010:

> Why take such a loved character and have him beat his wife to the point where he does not know how she got on the floor?
>
> Are you kidding me? What is that, and what was the point of reducing them to that level? Don't devoted readers of the series deserve better than that?

Another example is in response to Sister Souljah's last installment for *The Coldest Winter Ever* trilogy, *Life After Death: A Novel (The Coldest Winter Ever,* Book 2). One reader posted on Amazon.com on May 27, 2021:

> The first book was everything when I was young so I was so excited when I found out and waited patiently for the sequel. . . . I was not happy reading the first few chapters and I already guessed at how it would end. I really would've liked to see how Winter handled being back out in the world and how she interacted with the other characters from her past. I think this was a little bit of a wasted opportunity for Souljah to educate on the realities of life after prison for black women. . . . Souljah is an excellent storyteller and found a way to make me interested (and creeped out) to continue reading on to the end to see how she carried out the story. . . . I learned new things and saw things from a different perspective. I would recommend for people to read the book and tell them to keep reading because it is a pretty good read down the line and overall. I'm happy Souljah wrote this book for us Winter fans!

Ashley Antoinette's novel *Ethic* (a follow-up to her novel *Moth to a Flame*, 2010) was very popular when it was released in 2018, with readers remaining actively engaged in character analysis and discussion about the book and series on Goodreads.com. Just five years after its publication, on Goodreads, *Ethic* ranked 4.65 out of a 5-star rating, with 4,018 readers rating the book and 566 readers having posted reviews. Ethic is the male protagonist whose experiences as a father challenge him toward a drawback to street life. Reader Bookishrealm posted on May 29, 2022:

> Overall, this was a good installment to the overall series. I'm hoping that Ethic eventually does get a much deserved break because throughout the entirety of this book, I felt like he just kept losing. I want him to get that happily ever after, but for right now, it just seems unachievable. If you're looking for a fast-paced, thrilling, and dynamic series, I would definitely recommend checking this out.

These critical analyses are prevalent among reader comments and reviews on social platforms like Amazon.com and Goodreads.com for many street-lit titles. Brooks and Savage (2009) conducted a study on Amazon.com reader comments for street literature and learned that "the appeal of Street Lit narratives derives, at least in part, from readers' perceptions of literary quality (e.g., characters, storyline, theme) as well as the writer's ability to depict a reality that resonates with her readership (e.g., 'this book is how it is on the street')" (p. 52). It is apparent how the act of reading, regardless of what is being read, organically prompts readers to synthesize and assess what they read naturally. With street lit, these acts of literacy manifest as book club discourse, book networking and sharing between friends (and in social media, with authors, too), and commenting and reviewing books on book review websites and blogs. Decidedly, through these various acts of reading and information literacy practices, critical analysis becomes a natural part of the reading of the reader's world.

THE READING LIBRARIAN

In this vein, librarians must be readers of not just street lit but as much literature as possible that rounds out the literary environment in which street lit thrives. This consideration means that librarians must be familiar with various literary traditions, such as African American literature (e.g., Chester Himes, James Baldwin, Zora Neale Hurston, Walter Mosley, Octavia Butler, Samuel Delaney, Edwidge Danticat, Touré, to name a few), Latino literature (e.g., Pam Muñoz Ryan, Sandra Cisneros, Junot Díaz, Piri Thomas, Cristina García, and Julia Alvarez), chick lit (which can be considered urban and women's fiction), lad lit, LGBTQIA+ literature, and contemporary fictions that depict urban settings (e.g., James Patterson, Zetta Elliott, E. Lynn Harris, Janet Evanovich, and Tananarive Due). Understanding that cultural and literary traditions are diasporic in scope is also essential.

Inclusivity and Representation in Street Lit

Thus, African American literature is not just stories about the streets or Black people in America; the genre also encompasses Caribbean, South American, African, Black European, and Canadian stories. The same understanding applies to all ethnic and cultural literature, chick lit, LGBTQIA+, and any other genre that intersects with street lit's themes and narratives. Street lit encompasses myriad genre spaces—diverse American experiences, gendered stories, and urban fictional narratives that are historical and contemporary, local, diasporic, and global.

When we, as librarians, are open-minded lifelong readers and learners by way of a reflexive- and inquiry-based stance that informs and impacts our professional practices and reading repertoires. When engaged with what our patrons read via readers' advisory and reference interviews, we are fortified to connect readers with a love and appreciation for reading and all its benefits. It is not only a matter of the librarian knowing many genres for the sake of being able to tell the patron, "We have this, and we have that," but such a repertoire is vital so that the librarian can parse out from the patron the depths of the patron's literary repertoire, to open up space to consider a fuller range of literary compatibilities and possibilities in what the patron wants to read.

Chapter 7

THE LITERATE LIBRARIAN

This book establishes the librarian's position not as an information expert who is an outsider to the community but as a patron of their own library workplace and service community, thus an insider to the community. As such, the librarian is a reader of the library, the collection, the patron, and most of all, of him- or herself as a community member and advocate. Indeed, as a reader of multiple figured worlds that intersect, interweave, and inform one upon the other, the librarian is a constant lifelong learner of the human condition via their social interactions in the form of the reference and readers' advisory interview (Mabry, 2004; Sisselman, 2009; Ross, Nilsen, and Radford, 2019). This multilayered world (Bartlett and Holland, 2002) encompasses the librarian's world of research, information retrieval, storage, management, social interaction, and cultural literacy practices. As a result, the librarian, as a de facto reader of the genre, is a representation of the notion of every reader for every book notion, per S. R. Ranganathan's law of library science: Every reader their book.

For example, for librarians who serve a city-based community, their sociocultural literacy is expressed in how they navigate their interactions in the streets. In the 'hood, everyone is a reader: a reader of the text, moods, tonalities, the weather, and the streets themselves. The inner-city librarian (and teacher, for that matter) is not exempt from this genus of information literacy.

It is not unheard of that public librarians witness and experience some of the themes laid out in street lit. As municipal employees in the public sphere, public librarians and teachers often witness threats and harassment, drug overdoses, sexual activity, riots, robbery, and even death in the library. Public libraries and schools are often venues where social issues erupt and manifest.

On the positive side, the library is a safe place for social development. For example, children become productive students because of time spent in the library; teens change from delinquents to college students or military personnel because of their consistent involvement with reading, library programming, and staff; adults are empowered to navigate bureaucratic city systems because of information or contacts obtained from the library; and on many occasions, people of all life stages obtain a lifelong reading habit because of their relationship with the library.

The dark and bright sides of public librarianship parallel similar themes in the street-lit genre. There are regular scenes in street-lit stories where characters engage in literacy activities, including reading books; writing letters, poems, and lyrics; and conducting research at the public library. Thus, it behooves us as librarians to be literate about our patrons' literature because, invariably, we are also characters in the very stories they read and in the very stories they live.

EPILOGUE
Street Lit's Enduring Legacy

This second edition of *The Readers' Advisory Guide to Street Literature* comes at a precariously intimidating time in our world's history, where ideas about acceptable reading material for every life stage have become oppressively imperialistic. For librarians, teachers, and other community-based educators, censorship, book banning, and artificial intelligence impact how we all respond to reading text, writing stories, and hearing collective voices in library collections.

This edition is being written during the year that marks the fiftieth anniversary of the birth of hip-hop, which was birthed on August 11, 1973. It has long been understood that hip-hop culture is comprised of five elements: DJing (musicianship), graffiti (cultural art), MCing (storytelling), b-boying (dance), and knowledge (building of identity). Street lit/urban fiction has long been regarded as the literature of hip-hop culture because the stories record the same street life chronicled in the music, murals, and text.

Urban fiction and hip-hop have been intertwined since their inception in the early 1970s, when DJ Kool Herc introduced the breakbeat into dance music that started hip-hop around the same time authors Donald Goines and Iceberg Slim were publishing the first wave of street-lit novels. Both art forms emerged simultaneously from the same communities, sharing a common goal of telling stories about the lived experiences of Black people. Street lit/urban fiction focuses on the struggles of city life, while hip-hop explores themes of poverty, violence, and social justice. Both hip-hop and street lit have been criticized for their depictions of violence and misogyny, but they have also been praised for their authenticity and for giving a voice to the voiceless.

Street-lit authors can be considered the literary bards of hip-hop culture, with their narratives serving as social protest fiction, revealing and exploring the sociocultural tensions between

Epilogue

contemporary twenty-first-century society and the bureaucratic forces that impact the circumstances of everyday citizens. Just as rappers and MCs musically tell the stories of their experiences and observations in their neighborhoods, street-lit authors do the same in literature. Even the pace and cadence of street-lit novels emulate the fast-paced rhythmic style of hip-hop MCs. Street lit's overall presentation chronicles the ongoing story of lived experience in urban-based communities.

Street lit/urban fiction has shaped America's early twenty-first-century literary culture by telling the stories of city-dwelling citizens' experiences of American life. Street lit carries a legacy of empowering authors' and readers' voices to be heard, counted, and validated. Over the years, street lit has experienced rapid change, with large publishing houses like Triple Crown Publications and Cash Money Content folding after a few prosperous years or moving to mainstream publishing houses like Simon & Schuster to establish imprints for the genre. Like hip-hop, street lit rides on an organic wave of continuous change and evolution, always carving new space for new authors and their stories.

In recent decades, street lit has also taken on multiple formats, from print to audio to digital to illustrated graphic novels. With books now available in various formats, street lit connects with the twenty-first-century readers' multimodal ways of engaging with text. The interactivity of the internet also affords conversation around characterization and story, with readers being able to interact with authors and one another on social media platforms where they can post commentary on the titles they have read. Indeed, one aspect of street lit's endurance as a literary force is the online interactions between readers and authors, where the direction and progress of characters and their stories have been influenced by direct reader feedback.

The legacy of street lit endures because it now has its own foundational canon that represents the narratives of urban-based citizens living a human life. Street lit's voice has created space for other kinds of urban-based literature to be highlighted during this early twenty-first century via genre-blending with literary genres such as speculative fiction, fantasy, and science fiction stories in urban settings. Street lit has increased young adult readership in public and school libraries. Its legacy will continue to inspire authors to approach literature creatively and authentically.

APPENDIX

Street/Urban Literature
A Foundational Collection

Note: Many of these titles are available in multiple formats: print, audio, digital, and illustrated.

TWENTIETH-CENTURY CLASSICS

Brown, Claude. 1965. *Manchild in the Promised Land.* New York: Macmillan.

Dunbar, Paul Laurence. [1902] 2011. *The Sport of the Gods.* New York: Signet.

*Goines, Donald. 1974. *Daddy Cool.* Los Angeles: Holloway House.

Goines, Donald. 1971. *Dopefiend.* Los Angeles: Holloway House.

Himes, Chester. 1960. *All Shot Up.* New York: Berkley.

Himes, Chester. 1959. *The Real Cool Killers.* New York: Avon.

Marshall, Paule. 1959. *Brown Girl, Brownstones.* New York: Feminist Press at the City University of New York.

Mosley, Walter. 1998. *Always Outnumbered, Always Outgunned.* New York: W. W. Norton.

Naylor, Gloria. 1982. *Women of Brewster Place.* New York: Penguin.

Petry, Ann. [1946] 1974. *The Street: A Novel.* Boston: Houghton Mifflin.

Puzo, Mario. 1965. *The Fortunate Pilgrim.* New York: Atheneum.

Puzo, Mario. 1969. *The Godfather.* New York: Putnam.

Roth, Henry. 1934. *Call It Sleep.* New York: Robert O. Ballou.

Ruark, Robert Chester. 1965. *The Honey Badger.* New York: Fawcett.

*Slim, Iceberg. 1969. *Pimp: The Story of My Life.* Los Angeles: Holloway House.

---

*Donald Goines and Iceberg Slim (Robert Beck) were the progenitors of the twenty-first-century street lit/urban fiction renaissance. Both were prolific in their craft, with Goines penning twelve novels and a four-volume series. Beck authored eight novels and two memoirs. Many hip-hop artists credit Goines and Slim in their lyrics, and urban fiction authors credit the authors with influencing their craft.

Slim, Iceberg. [1967] 2014. *Trick Baby: The Story of a White Negro.* New York: Cash Money Content.

Thomas, Piri. [1967] 1997. *Down These Mean Streets.* New York: Alfred A. Knopf.

Wright, Richard. 1945. *Black Boy.* New York: Harper and Brothers.

Wright, Richard. 1940. *Native Son.* New York: Harper and Brothers.

X, Malcolm, as told to Alex Haley. 1965. *The Autobiography of Malcolm X.* New York: Grove Press.

TWENTY-FIRST-CENTURY CLASSICS

Ashley and JaQuavis. 2008–2020. *The Cartel* [volumes 1–10]. New York: Urban Books.

Ashley and JaQuavis. 2005. *Diary of a Street Diva.* New York: Urban Books.

Blue, Treasure E. 2004. *Harlem Girl Lost: A Novel.* New York: Ballantine Books.

Blue, Treasure E. 2007. *A Street Girl Named Desire: A Novel.* New York: Ballantine Books.

Chunichi. 2004–2009. *A Gangster's Girl* [volumes 1–4]. New York: Urban Books.

Clark, Wahida. 2010. *The Golden Hustla.* New York: Grand Central.

Clark, Wahida. 2022. *The Golden Hustla 2.* Fairburn, GA: Wahida Clark Presents Publishing.

Clark, Wahida. 2002–2019. *Thugs and the Women Who Love Them* [*Thug* Series, volumes 1–7]. New York: Wahida Clark Presents Publishing.

Foye, K'wan. 2012–2021. *Animal* [volumes 1–5]. New York: Cash Money Content.

Foye, K'wan. 2005. *Hoodlum: A Novel.* New York: St. Martin's Griffin.

Holmes, Shannon. 2000. *B-More Careful: A Novel.* New York: Teri Woods Publishing.

King, Joy Deja. 2004–2022. *Bitch* [volumes 1–11]. Collierville, TN: King Productions.

Quiñonez, Ernesto. 2000. *Bodega Dreams: A Novel.* New York: Vintage Contemporaries.

Sapphire. 1996. *Push.* New York: Alfred A. Knopf.

Slim, Iceberg. [1978] 1998. *Doom Fox.* New York: Grove/Atlantic.

Souljah, Sister. 1999. *The Coldest Winter Ever.* New York: Atria.

Souljah, Sister. 2014. *A Deeper Love Inside: The Porsche Santiaga Story.* New York: Atria.

Souljah, Sister. 2021. *Life after Death* [*The Coldest Winter Ever,* Part 2]. New York: Atria.

Souljah, Sister. 2008–2016. *Midnight: A Gangster Love Story* [trilogy]. New York: Atria.

Stringer, Vickie M. 2009. *Let That Be the Reason.* Brooklyn, NY: UpStream/A&B Publishing.

Teague, Kwame, and Teri Woods. 2007–2011. *Dutch* [trilogy]. New York: Grand Central Publishing.

Turner, Nikki. 2003–2011. *A Hustler's Wife* [trilogy]. Columbus, OH: Triple Crown.

Tyree, Omar. 2005. *Boss Lady.* New York: Simon & Schuster.

Tyree, Omar. 1993. *Flyy Girl.* Washington, DC: Mars Productions.

Woods, Teri. 1994–2008. *True to the Game* [trilogy]. New York: Meow Meow Teri Woods Publishing.

STREET LIT: THE CONTEMPORARY COLLECTION

Aaron, Relentless. 2001. *Push.* New York: St. Martin's.

Antoinette, Ashley. 2018–2019. *Ethic* [volumes 1–6]. Utica, MI: Ashley Antoinette, Inc.

Antoinette, Ashley. [2010] 2020. *Moth to a Flame* [10th anniversary edition]. New York: Urban Books.

Aquino, Melissa Coss. 2023. *Carmen and Grace: A Novel.* London: Head of Zeus.

Artemis, Black. 2004. *Explicit Content.* New York: Penguin.

Ashley and JaQuavis. 2012. *Kiss Kiss, Bang Bang.* New York: Urban Books.

Appendix

Brown, Tracy. 2003. *Black: A Street Tale.* Columbus, OH: Triple Crown.

Brown, Tracy. 2007. *White Lines: A Novel.* New York: St. Martin's Griffin.

Coleman, Ashley, and JaQuavis Coleman. 2011–2013. *Murderville* [trilogy]. New York: Cash Money Content.

Coleman, JaQuavis. 2013. *The Day the Streets Stood Still.* Wyandanch, NY: Urban Books.

Ervin, Keisha. 2004. *Chyna Black.* Columbus, OH: Triple Crown.

Frisby, Mister Mann. 2005. *Wifebeater.* New York: Riverhead Trade.

Glenn, Roy. 2015–2020. *The Mike Black Saga* [various titles: volumes 1–32]. New York: Escapism Entertainment.

Gray, Erick S., Anthony Whyte, and Mark Anthony. 2009. *The Streets of New York* [trilogy]. New York: Augustus.

Holmes, Shannon. 2007. *Dirty Game.* New York: St. Martin's Griffin.

Holmes, Shannon. 2004. *Never Go Home Again: A Novel.* New York: Atria.

Hunt, LaJill, Treasure Hernandez, and Various Authors. 2007–2023. *Around the Way Girls* [volumes 1–12]. New York: Urban Books.

Jones, Solomon. 2004. *The Bridge: A Novel.* New York: Minotaur.

Jones, Solomon. 2007. *C.R.E.A.M.* New York: St. Martin's Griffin.

Jones, Solomon. 2001. *Pipe Dream: A Novel.* New York: Villard/Strivers Row.

Jones, Solomon. 2005. *Ride or Die.* New York: Minotaur.

Karrington, Blake. 2021. *The King of the South.* Charlotte, NC: Karrington Media Group.

Karrington, Blake. 2022. *The King of the South 2: Every King Needs a Queen.* Charlotte, NC: Karrington Media Group.

K'wan. 2003. *Gangsta.* New York: St. Martin's Griffin.

K'wan. 2006. *Hood Rat: A Novel.* New York: St. Martin's Griffin.

K'wan. 2003. *Road Dawgz.* Columbus, OH: Triple Crown.

K'wan. 2004. *Street Dreams.* New York: St. Martin's Griffin.

Mill, Meek. 2013. *Tony Story.* GA: G Street Chronicles.

Rivera, Jeff. 2004. *Forever My Lady.* New York: Grand Central.

Robbins, Will. 2009. *Ice.* Columbus, OH: Triple Crown.

Shakur, Sanyika. 2009. *T.H.U.G. L.I.F.E.* New York: Grove Press.

Stringer, Vickie M. 2006–2010. *Dirty Red* [trilogy]. New York: Atria.

Stringer, Vickie M. 2004. *Imagine This.* Columbus, OH: Triple Crown.

Swinson, Kiki. 2004–2022. *Wifey* [volumes 1–4]. Bellport, NY: Kensington Books.

Turner, Nikki. 2004. *A Project Chick.* Columbus, OH: Triple Crown.

Turner, Nikki, Treasure Hernandez, and Various Authors. 2005–2022. *Girls from da Hood* [volumes 1–14]. New York: Urban Books.

Weber, Carl, with Eric Pete, Treasure Hernandez, C. N. Phillips, and La Jill Hunt. 2012–2024. *The Family Business* [volumes 1–6]. New York: Urban Books.

Williams, KaShamba. 2003. *Blinded: An Urban Tale!* Columbus, OH: Triple Crown.

Williams, KaShamba. 2004. *Grimey: The Sequel to Blinded.* Columbus, OH: Triple Crown.

Williams, KaShamba. 2005. *Driven: When You Can't Take Anything Else.* New York: Urban Books.

Zane. 1998. *Addicted.* New York: Atria.

LGBTQIA TITLES

Britt, A. C. 2007. *London Reign.* New York: GhettoHeat.

Brown, Laurinda D. 2007. *Strapped.* New York: Urban Books.

Collins, D. L. 2007. *A Stud's Love: A Lesbian Drama.* Bloomington, IN: iUniverse.

Hall, Reginald L. 2007. *In Love with a Thug.* New York: Strebor.

Ish, Mr. 2019. *Element of Surprise: An Urban Thriller.* Newark, NJ: Str8line Publications.

Jackson, Missy. 2009. *Cheetah: Always Be Ahead of the Hustle.* East Orange, NJ: Wahida Clark Presents.

Kahari, Asante. 2004. *Homo Thug.* New York: Gotham City.

Kahari, Asante. 2009. *Homo Thug,* Part 2. New York: Harlem Book Center.

Meadows, Damon, and Jason Poole. 2006. *Convict's Candy*. New York: GhettoHeat.

N'Tyse. 2007. *My Secrets Your Lies*. Dallas, TX: A Million Thoughts.

Nikki-Michelle. 2017. *Bi-Sensual*. New York: Urban Renaissance Books.

Nero, Clarence. 2006. *Three Sides to Every Story: A Novel*. New York: Harlem Moon.

Panfil, Vanessa R. 2017. *The Gang's All Queer: The Lives of Gay Gang Members*. New York University Press.

Pope, M. T. 2009. *Both Sides of the Fence*. New York: Urban Books.

Pope, M. T. 2010. *Both Sides of the Fence 2*. New York: Urban Books.

Pope, M. T. 2012. *A Clean Up Man*. New York: Urban Books.

Pope, M. T. 2019. *Hustling on the Down Low*. New York: Urban Books.

Racheal, Christine. 2010. *Trickery*. Columbus, OH: Triple Crown.

Sidi. 2006. *The Lesbian's Wife*. New York: Harlem Book Center.

Vernon, Dwayne. 2010. *Roman*. MD: Norcarjo.

Wash, C. 2021. *Hersband Material 2: Jailhouse Butch*. Owings Mills, MD: Cartel Publications.

Wilson, Rashima. 2020. *Exposure of a HomoThug: A Ratchet City Tale*. New York: RKW Publishing.

YOUNG ADULT URBAN FICTION

Booth, Coe. 2008. *Kendra*. New York: Push.

Booth, Coe. 2006. *Tyrell*. New York: Push.

Buckhanon, Kalisha. 2004. *Upstate*. New York: St. Martin's Griffin.

Dupree, Kia. 2010. *Damaged*. New York: Grand Central.

Flake, Sharon G. 2005. *Bang!* New York: Hyperion/Jump at the Sun.

Flake, Sharon G. 2003. *Begging for Change*. New York: Hyperion/ Jump at the Sun.

Flake, Sharon G. 2001. *Money Hungry*. New York: Hyperion/ Jump at the Sun.

Flake, Sharon G. 1998. *The Skin I'm In.* New York: Hyperion/Jump at the Sun.

Flake, Sharon G. 2004. *Who Am I without Him?* New York: Hyperion/Jump at the Sun.

Flake, Sharon G. 2010. *You Don't Even Know My Name: Stories and Poems about Boys.* New York: Hyperion/Jump at the Sun.

Franklin, Johnny, Jr. 2021. *The Struggle: Striving to Survive.*

Frost, Helen. 2003. *Keesha's House.* New York: Farrar, Straus, and Giroux.

McDonald, Janet. 2004. *Brother Hood.* New York: Farrar, Straus, and Giroux.

McDonald, Janet. 2006. *Chill Wind.* New York: Farrar, Straus, and Giroux.

McDonald, Janet. 2000. *Project Girl.* Berkeley, CA: University of California Press.

McDonald, Janet. 2003. *Twists and Turns.* New York: Farrar, Straus, and Giroux.

Myers, Walter Dean. 2013. *Darius and Twig.* New York: Amistad Books for Young Readers.

Myers, Walter Dean. 2009. *Dope Sick.* New York: Amistad.

Myers, Walter Dean. 1999. *Monster.* New York: Amistad.

Myers, Walter Dean. 2006. *Street Love.* New York: Amistad.

Myers, Walter Dean, and Christopher Myers. 2005. *Autobiography of My Dead Brother.* New York: Amistad.

Reynolds, Jason. 2014. *When I Was the Greatest.* New York: Amistad Books for Young Readers.

Thomas, Angie. 2017. *The Hate U Give.* New York: Balzer+Bray.

Thomas, Angie. 2019. *On the Come Up.* New York: Balzer+Bray.

Zoboi, Ibi. 2017. *American Street.* New York: Balzer+Bray.

YOUNG ADULT SERIES

Daniels, Babygirl. 2009. *Baby Girl Drama* [volumes 1–4]. New York: Urban Books.

Divine, L. 2006–2019. *Drama High* [volumes 1–19]. New York: Kensington-Teen/Dafina.

Langan, Paul, and Various Authors. 2001–2021. *Bluford High* [volumes 1–23]. New York: Scholastic.

Lee, Darrien. 2008–2010. *Denim Diaries* [volumes 1–5]. New York: Urban Books.

Moore, Stephanie Perry. 2009. *Beta Gamma Pi* [volumes 1–5]. New York: Kensington-Teen/Dafina.

Sewell, Earl, Celeste O. Norfleet, and Various Authors. 2007–2014. *Kimani Tru* [volumes 1–19]. New York: Harlequin Kimani TRU.

Simone, Ni-Ni. 2008–2013. *Ni-Ni Girl Chronicles* [volumes 1–7]. New York: Dafina.

NONFICTION (POETRY)

Ardis, Angela. 2009. *Inside a Thug's Heart.* New York: Dafina.

Brown, Jericho. 2008. *Please.* Kalamazoo, MI: New Issues Poetry and Prose.

Browne, Mahogany L. 2022. *Vinyl Moon.* New York: Crown Books for Young Readers.

Hodge, Chinaka. 2016. *Dated Emcees (City Lights/Sister Spit).* San Francisco, CA: City Lights Publishers.

Holter, Jessica. 2000. *Speak the Unspeakable.* Oakland, CA: GGB Literary Entertainment.

Lewis, Miles Marshall. 2021. *Promise That You Will Sing About Me: The Power and Poetry of Kendrick Lamar.* New York: St. Martin's Press.

Medina, Tony, and Louis Reyes Rivera, eds. 2001. *Bum Rush the Page: A Def Poetry Slam.* New York: Three Rivers.

Myers, Walter Dean. 2006. *Street Love.* New York: Amistad.

Park, Ishle Yi. 2021. *Angel and Hannah: A Novel in Verse.* New York: One World.

Reynolds. Jason. 2017. *Long Way Down.* New York: Atheneum/ Caitlyn Dlouhy Books.

Scott, Jill. 2005. *The Moments, the Minutes, the Hours: The Poetry of Jill Scott.* New York: St. Martin's Griffin.

Shakur, Tupac. 1999. *The Rose That Grew from Concrete.* New York: MTV/Pocket Books.

Smith, Patricia. 1993. *Close to Death: Poems.* Cambridge, MA: Zoland.

Williams, Saul. 2006. *The Dead Emcee Scrolls: The Lost Teachings of Hip-Hop.* New York: MTV.

NONFICTION (INCLUDING BIOGRAPHIES/MEMOIRS)

Allen, Eddie B., Jr. 2008. *Low Road: The Life and Legacy of Donald Goines.* New York: St. Martin's Griffin.

Anderson, Elijah. 1999. *Code of the Street: Decency, Violence and the Moral Life of the Inner City.* New York: W. W. Norton.

Betts, R. Dwayne. 2009. *A Question of Freedom: A Memoir of Learning, Survival, and Coming of Age in Prison.* New York: Penguin/Avery.

Bourgois, Phillippe. 1995. *In Search of Respect: Selling Crack in El Barrio.* Cambridge: Cambridge University Press.

Bourgois, Phillippe. 2009. *Righteous Dopefiend.* Berkeley, CA: University of California Press.

Canada, Geoffrey. 1995. *Fish, Knife, Stick, Gun: A Personal History of Violence in America.* Boston: Beacon.

Dash, Leon. 1997. *Rosa Lee: A Mother and Her Family in Urban America.* New York: Plume.

Davis, Sampson, George Jenkins, and Rameck Hunt, with Sharon M. Draper. 2006. *We Beat the Street: How a Friendship Pact Led to Success.* New York: Puffin.

DMX, as told to Smokey D. Fontaine. 2003. *E.A.R.L.: The Autobiography of DMX.* New York: HarperCollins.

50 Cent, with Kris Ex. 2005. *From Pieces to Weight: Once upon a Time in Southside Queens.* New York: MTV.

Jasper, Kenji. 2006. *The House on Childress Street: A Memoir.* New York: Harlem Moon.

Jay-Z (Shawn Carter). 2011. *Decoded.* New York: One World.

Jones, LeAlan, and Lloyd Newman, with David Isay. 1998. *Our America: Life and Death on the South Side of Chicago.* New York: Scribner.

Kenner, Rob. 2021. *The Marathon Don't Stop: The Life and Times of Nipsey Hussle*. New York: Atria.

Kotlowitz, Alex. 1992. *There Are No Children Here: The Story of Two Boys Growing Up in the Other America*. New York: Anchor Books.

LeBlanc, Adrian Nicole. 2003. *Random Family: Love, Drugs, Trouble, and Coming of Age in the Bronx*. New York: Scribner.

McCall, Nathan. 1995. *Makes Me Wanna Holler: A Young Black Man in America*. New York: Vintage.

Morris, DaShaun "Jiwe." 2008. *War of the Bloods in My Veins: A Street Soldier's March toward Redemption*. New York: Scribner.

Pearson, Felicia "Snoop." 2007. *Grace after Midnight: A Memoir*. New York: Grand Central.

S., Tina, and Jamie Pastor Bolnick. 2000. *Living at the Edge of the World: A Teenager's Survival in the Tunnels of Grand Central Station*. New York: St. Martin's Press.

Sanchez, Ivan. 2008. *Next Stop: Growing Up Wild-Style in the Bronx*. New York: Touchstone.

Sanchez, Reymundo. 2000. *My Bloody Life: The Making of a Latin King*. Chicago: Chicago Review Press.

Sanchez, Reymundo, and Sonia Rodriguez. 2008. *Lady Q: The Rise and Fall of a Latin Queen*. Chicago: Chicago Review Press.

Shakur, Sanyika. 1994. *Monster: The Autobiography of an L. A. Gang Member*. New York: Grove Press.

Shalhoup, Mara. 2010. *BMF: The Rise and Fall of Big Meech and the Black Mafia Family*. New York: St. Martin's Press.

Simon, David, and Edward Burns. 1997. *The Corner: A Year in the Life of an Inner-City Neighborhood*. New York: Broadway.

Slim, Iceberg. 1971. *The Naked Soul of Iceberg Slim: Robert Beck's Real Story*. Los Angeles, CA: Holloway House.

Souljah, Sister. 1995. *No Disrespect*. New York: Vintage.

Thomas-El, Salome, with Cecil Murphey. 2004. *I Choose to Stay: A Black Teacher Refuses to Desert the Inner City*. New York: Kensington.

Wayne, Lil. 2016. *Gone 'Til November: A Journal of Rikers Island*. New York: Blink Publishing.

Williams, Stanley Tookie. 2007. *Blue Rage, Black Redemption: A Memoir*. New York: Touchstone.

REFERENCES

Abdul, A. 2022. "I'm the Lucky One." *Knowledge Quest* 51, no. 1: 16–21.

Agosto, D. E. 2022. "Reflections on Adolescent Literacy as Sociocultural Practice." *Information and Learning Science* 123, no. 11/12: 723–37. https://doi.org/10.1108/ILS-02-2022-0013.

Aiex, Nola Kortner. 1993. "Bibliotherapy." Eric Digest ED357333. Eric Clearinghouse on Reading, English, and Communication. https://eric.ed.gov/?id=ED357333.

Alessio, Amy. 2004. "Respect for the Future: Making Space for Older Teens." In *Serving Older Teens*, edited by Sheila B. Anderson Mikkelson, 87–102. Westport, CT: Libraries Unlimited.

American Library Association. 2021. "Code of Ethics." American Library Association. www.ala.org/tools/ethics.

Anderson, Elijah. 1999. *Code of the Street: Decency, Violence and the Moral Life of the Inner City.* New York: W. W. Norton.

Anderson, Elijah, ed. 2008. *Against the Wall: Poor, Young, Black, and Male.* The City in the Twenty-First Century. Philadelphia: University of Pennsylvania Press.

Anderson, Elijah. 2022. *Black in White Space: The Enduring Impact of Color in Everyday Life.* Chicago: University of Chicago Press.

Andrews, V. C. 1979. *Flowers in the Attic.* New York: Simon & Schuster.

Appleyard, J. A. 1991. *Becoming a Reader: The Experience of Fiction from Childhood to Adulthood.* Cambridge: Cambridge University Press.

Ault, P. B. 2006. "The Later City Novel: Narrative, Form and Agenda." MPhil thesis, Swansea University (United Kingdom). ProQuest Dissertations and Theses Global.

Balaji, Murali. 2012. "The Construction of 'Street Credibility' in Atlanta's Hip-Hop Music Scene: Analyzing the Role of Cultural Gatekeepers." *Critical Studies in Media Communication* 29, no. 4: 313–30. https://doi.org/10.1080/15295036.2012.665997.

References

Bartlett, Lesley, and Dorothy Holland. 2002. "Theorizing the Space of Literacy Practices." *Ways of Knowing Journal* 2, no. 1 (January): 10–22.

Barton, David, and Mary Hamilton. 1998. *Local Literacies: Reading and Writing in One Community*. London: Routledge.

Bottigheimer, Ruth B. 2009. *Fairy Tales: A New History*. Albany: State University of New York Press.

Boyd, K. C. 2018. "K. C. Boyd Talks Street Lit | Banned Books Week 2018." *School Library Journal*, YouTube video, 3:16, August 30. https://youtu.be/pZnR8xAPZso.

Brooks, Wanda, and Lorraine Savage. 2009. "Critiques and Controversies of Street Literature: A Formidable Literary Genre." *ALAN Review* 36, no. 2 (Winter): 48–55. https://doi.org/10.21061/alan.v36i2.a.6.

Bruner, Jerome. 1986. *Actual Minds, Possible Worlds*. Cambridge, MA: Harvard University Press.

Buvala, K. Sean. [2007] 2022. "Two Plus One Is Greater than Three: The Presence of the Number 3 in Folktales." Storyteller.net, October 15. https://storyteller.net/two-plus-one-is-greater-than-three-the-presence-of-the-number-3-in-fairytales-and-folklore/.

Campbell, Donna M. 2017. "Naturalism in American Literature." Literary Movements, Department of English, Washington State University. Last modified March 8. https://public.wsu.edu/~campbelld/amlit/natural.htm.

Cannon, Peter. 2018. "Rethinking Bibliotherapy: A Neurorhetoric Narratology Model for Addiction Treatment." *Health Information and Libraries Journal* 35, no. 4 (December): 331–35. https://doi.org/10.1111/hir.12239.

Caramanica, Jon. 2005. "Hip-Hop's Raiders of the Lost Archives." *New York Times*, June 26. https://web.archive.org/web/20140410093712/http://www.nytimes.com/2005/06/26/arts/music/26jon.html.

Chance, Rosemary. 2008. *Young Adult Literature in Action: A Librarian's Guide*. Santa Barbara, CA: Libraries Unlimited.

Chiles, Nick. 2006. "Their Eyes Were Reading Smut." *New York Times*, January 4. www.nytimes.com/2006/01/04/opinion/their-eyes-were-reading-smut.html.

References

Cochran-Smith, Marilyn, and Susan L. Lytle. 2009. *Inquiry as Stance: Practitioner Research for the Next Generation.* New York: Teachers College Press.

Compton-Lilly, Catherine. 2007. *Re-Reading Families: The Literate Lives of Urban Children, Four Years Later.* New York: Teachers College Press.

Cruz, José. 2015. "Tapping into the WONDER & MAGIC of Literature." *Scholastic Administrator* 14, no. 2: 21.

de Leon, Aya. 2019. "It's Time for Urban Fiction to Get Some Literary Respect." CrimeReads, July 8. https://crimereads.com/its-time-for-urban-fiction-to-get-some-literary-respect/.

Dimitriadis, George. 2003. *Friendship, Cliques, and Gangs: Young Black Men Coming of Age in Urban America.* New York: Teachers College Press.

Doyle, Miranda. 2005. "Sex, Drugs, and Drama: More Books like 'The Coldest Winter Ever.'" *VOYA: Voice of Youth Advocates Magazine* 28, no. 3: 190–93.

Evans, S. A. 2019. "'Book Nerds' United: The Reading Lives of Diverse Adolescents at the Public Library." *The International Journal of Information, Diversity, & Inclusion* 3, no. 2 (2019): 40–62. https://doi.org/10.33137/ijidi.v3i2.32589.

Ferriss, Suzanne, and Mallory Young, eds. 2005. *Chick Lit: The New Woman's Fiction.* New York: Routledge.

Gates, Henry Louis. 2004. "The Black, White of Vernacular." *Tulsa (OK) World,* New York Times Syndicate, October 17. https://tinyurl.com/5efymk7y.

Gibson, Simone. 2016. "Adolescent African American Girls as Engaged Readers: Challenging Stereotypical Images of Black Womanhood through Urban Fiction." *Journal of Negro Education,* 85, no. 3: 212–24. https://doi.org/10.7709/jnegroeducation.85.3.0212.

Gifford, Justin. 2015. *Street Poison: The Biography of Iceberg Slim.* New York: Doubleday.

Gorman, Michele Elizabeth, and Tricia Ann Suellentrop. 2009. *Connecting Young Adults and Libraries: A How-To-Do-It Manual,* 4th ed. New York: Neal-Schuman.

References

Graaff, Kristina, and Vanessa Irvin. 2015. "The Rise of Urban Fiction." In *Black Culture and Experience: Contemporary Issues,* edited by Venise T. Berry, Anita Fleming-Rife, and Ayo Dayo, 195–206. New York: Peter Lang.

Guerra, Stephanie F. 2012. "Using Urban Fiction to Engage At-Risk and Incarcerated Youths in Literacy Instruction." *Journal of Adolescent and Adult Literacy* 55, no. 5 (February): 385–94. https://doi.org/10.1002/JAAL.00047.

Hakutani, Yoshinobu, and Robert Butler, eds. 1995. *The City in African-American Literature.* Vancouver, BC: Fairleigh Dickinson University Press.

Hansberry, Lorraine. 1959. *A Raisin in the Sun.* New York: Random House.

Haywood, Antoine. 2021. "Cover Art: A Reflection on Afrofuturistic Album Covers, Funk Music, and Black American Identity Formation." *Journal of Popular Music Studies* 33, no. 3 (September): 26–30. https://doi.org/10.1525/jpms.2021.33.3.26.

Holmes, Shannon. 2004. *Never Go Home Again.* New York: Atria Books.

Hua, Anh. 2006. "Memory and Cultural Trauma: Women of Color in Literature and Film." PhD diss., York University.

Irvin, Vanessa. 2009. "Precious—The Response." *Street Literature* (blog), December 14. https://streetliterature.blogspot.com/2009/12/precious-movie-written-11282009.html.

Irvin, Vanessa. 2012. "Reading in Mirrors: Using Street Literature to Facilitate Practitioner Inquiry with Urban Public Service Librarians." EdD diss., University of Pennsylvania.

Iser, Wolfgang. 1978. *The Act of Reading: A Theory of Aesthetic Response.* Baltimore, MD: John Hopkins University Press.

Iser, Wolfgang. 1980. "Texts and Readers." *Discourse Processes* 3, no. 4: 327–43.

Jones, Charisse. 2015. "Kevin Powell Writes a Searing yet Uplifting Memoir." *USA Today,* November 12. www.usatoday.com/story/life/books/2015/11/12/the-education-of-kevin-powell-a-boys-journey-into-manhood/73815622/.

Jones, Gerald Everett. 2010. *Boychick Lit* (blog). www.boychiklit.com.

References

Kumasi, Kafi. 2010. "Cultural Inquiry: A Framework for Engaging Youth of Color in the Library." *Journal of Research on Libraries and Young Adults* 1, no. 1 (November). www.yalsa.ala.org/jrlya/2010/11.

Landay, Eileen. 2004. "Performance as the Foundation for a Secondary School Literacy Program: A Bakhtinian Perspective." In *Bakhtinian Perspectives on Language, Literacy and Learning*, edited by Arnetha F. Ball and Sarah Warshauer Freedman, 107–28. Cambridge: Cambridge University Press.

Lavenne, François-Xavier, Virginie Renard, and François Tollet. 2005. "Fiction, between Inner Life and Collective Memory: A Methodological Reflection." *New Arcadia Review* 3. www.scribd.com/document/244118927/Fiction-Between-Inner-Life-and-Collective-Memory.

Long, Elizabeth. 2003. *Book Clubs: Women and the Uses of Reading in Everyday Life*. Chicago: University of Chicago Press.

Luu, Chi. 2020. "Black English Matters." *JSTOR Daily*, February 12. https://daily.jstor.org/black-english-matters/.

Lyubymova, Svitlana, and National Linguistic University, Kyiv, Ukraine. 2021. "American Dream Revisited: A Media Discourse Representation in Cognitive-Linguistic Perspective." *Rupkatha Journal on Interdisciplinary Studies in Humanities* 13, no. 4: 1–15. https://doi.org/10.21659/rupkatha.v13n4.27.

Mabry, Celia Hales. 2004. "The Reference Interview as Partnership: An Examination of Librarian, Library User, and Social Interaction." *Reference Librarian* 40, no. 83–84: 41–56. https://doi.org/10.1300/J120v40n83_05.

Marshall, Elizabeth, Jeanine Staples, and Simone Gibson. 2009. "Ghetto Fabulous: Reading Representations of Black Adolescent Femininity in Contemporary Urban Street Fiction." *Journal of Adolescent and Adult Literacy* 53, no. 1 (September): 28–36.

Martin, Philip. 2014. "Trends in Migration to the U.S." PRB, May 19. www.prb.org/resources/trends-in-migration-to-the-u-s/.

McFadden, Bernice L. 2010. "Black Writers in a Ghetto of the Publishing Industry's Making." *Washington Post*, June 26. www.washingtonpost.com/wp-dyn/content/article/2010/06/25/AR2010062504125.html.

Morris, Vanessa. 2007. "Inner-City Teens Do Read: Their Lives Represented in Urban Street Fiction." Paper presented at Beyond the Book: Contemporary Cultures of Reading, University of Birmingham, Birmingham, UK, August 31–September 3. www.slideshare.net/vanirvinmorris/inner-city-teens-do-read.

Morris, Vanessa, Sandra Hughes-Hassell, Denise E. Agosto, and Darren T. Cottman. 2006. "Street Lit: Flying Off Teen Bookshelves in Philadelphia Public Libraries." *Young Adult Library Services* 5, no. 1: 16–23.

Newman, Katherine S. 2000. *No Shame in My Game: The Working Poor in the Inner City*. New York: Alfred A. Knopf.

Nishikawa, Kinohi. 2020. "Black Women Readers and the Uses of Urban Fiction." In *Are You Entertained? Black Popular Culture in the Twenty-First Century*, edited by Simone C. Drake and Dwan K. Henderson. Durham, NC: Duke University Press.

Nix, Taylor. 2009. "Ashley and JaQuavis Crack New York Times Bestsellers List." Urban Book Source: Your Online Authority for Urban Literature, December. http://theubs.com/features/ashley-jaquavis.php?comments_page=6 (website discontinued).

Owens, Lily, ed. 1981. *The Complete Brothers Grimm Fairy Tales*. New York: Avenel/Crown.

Pernice, Ronda Racha. 2010. "Black Books Are Bigger than 'Ghetto Lit.'" Grio, September 23. www.thegrio.com/entertainment/why-blacks-should-care-about-the-book-industrys-future.php (web page discontinued).

Petry, Ann. [1946] 1974. *The Street: A Novel*. Boston: Houghton Mifflin.

Pettegree, Andrew, ed. 2017. *Broadsheets: Single-Sheet Publishing in the First Age of Print*. Leiden, Netherlands: Brill. www.jstor.org/stable/10.1163/j.ctv2gjwnfd.

Radway, Janice A. 1991. *Reading the Romance: Women, Patriarchy, and Popular Literature*, 2nd ed. Chapel Hill: University of North Carolina Press.

Rafferty, Terrence. 2008. "Shelley's Daughters." *New York Times*, October 24. www.nytimes.com/2008/10/26/books/review/Rafferty-t.html.

References

Reference and User Services Association. 2023. *Guidelines for Behavioral Performance of Reference and Information Service Providers*. Chicago: American Library Association. www.ala.org/rusa/resources/guidelines/guidelinesbehavioral.

Rosenblatt, Louise M. [1978] 1994. *The Reader, the Text, the Poem: The Transactional Theory of the Literary Work*. Carbondale: Southern Illinois University Press.

Rosenblatt, Louise M. 1983. *Literature as Exploration*. New York: Noble.

Rosenblatt, Louise M. 1986. "The Aesthetic Transaction." *Journal of Aesthetic Education* 20, no. 4 (Winter): 122–28. https://doi.org/10.2307/3332615.

Ross, Catherine Sheldrick, Kirsti Nilsen, and Marie L. Radford. 2019. *Conducting the Reference Interview: A How-To-Do-It Manual for Librarians*, 3rd ed. Chicago: ALA Neal-Schuman.

Saffou, Mazin Bashire. 2014. "American Dreams: Portrayals of Race, Class, and 21st Century Capitalism in David Simon and Ed Burns' The Wire." Master's thesis, University of Regina (Canada). ProQuest Dissertations Publishing.

Shange, Ntozake. 1977. *For Colored Girls Who Have Considered Suicide/When the Rainbow Is Enuf*. New York: Macmillan.

Shepard, Leslie. 1973. *The History of Street Literature: The Story of Broadside Ballads, Chapbooks, Proclamations, News-Sheets, Election Bills, Tracts, Pamphlets, Cocks, Catchpennies, and Other Ephemera*. Detroit, MI: Singing Tree Press.

Shipler, David K. 2005. *The Working Poor: Invisible in America*. New York: Vintage.

Sisselman, Peggy. 2009. "Exploiting the Social Style of Patrons to Improve Their Satisfaction with the Reference Interview." *Library Review* 58, no. 2: 124–33. https://doi.org/10.1108/00242530910936943.

Slim, Iceberg. [1978] 1998. *Doom Fox*. New York: Grove/Atlantic.

Smith, Duncan. 2000. "Talking with Readers: A Competency Based Approach to Readers' Advisory Service." *Reference and User Services Quarterly* 40, no. 2 (Winter): 135–42.

Smithsonian American Art Museum. 2015. "The Second Great Migration." The American Experience in the Classroom. https://americanexperience.si.edu/wp-content/uploads/2015/02/The-Second-Great-Migration.pdf.

References

Stallman, Robert Wooster. 1955. "Stephen Crane's Revision of *Maggie: A Girl of the Streets." American Literature* 26, no. 4 (January): 528–36.

Statista. 2023. "Largest Urban Agglomerations Worldwide in 2022, by Population." www.statista.com/statistics/912263/population-of-urban-agglomerations-worldwide/ (page content changed).

Sumara, Dennis J. 1996. *Private Readings in Public: Schooling the Literary Imagination.* New York: Peter Lang.

Sweeney, Megan. 2010. *Reading Is My Window: Books and the Art of Reading in Women's Prisons.* Chapel Hill: University of North Carolina Press.

Thomas-Bailey, Carlene. 2011. "Is 'Urban Fiction' Defined by Its Subject—or the Skin Colour of Its Author?" *Guardian,* November 3. www.theguardian.com/books/2011/nov/03/black-urban-fiction-american.

"thyung." 2005. Urban Dictionary. www.urbandictionary.com/authorphp?author=thyung (web page discontinued).

Van Fleet, Connie. 2008. "Education for Readers' Advisory Service in Library and Information Science Programs: Challenges and Opportunities." *Reference and User Services Quarterly* 47, no. 3 (2008), 224–29. https://doi.org/10.5860/rusq.47n3.224.

Venkatesh, Sudhir A. 2006. *Off the Books: The Underground Economy of the Urban Poor.* Cambridge, MA: Harvard University Press.

Verden, Claire E. 2012. "Reading Culturally Relevant Literature Aloud to Urban Youths with Behavioral Challenges." *Journal of Adolescent and Adult Literacy* 55, no. 7 (April): 619–28. https://doi.org/10.1002/JAAL.00073.

Warner, Judith. 2007. "A Warm Welcome for 'Dad Lit.'" *Opinionator* (blog), *New York Times,* May 17. http://opinionator.blogs.nytimes.com/2007/05/17/a-warm-welcome-for-dad-lit/?apage=3.

Wilson, William Julius. 2009. *More than Just Race: Being Black and Poor in the Inner City.* New York: W. W. Norton.

Wise, Alana. 2023. "Quan Millz Is Out to Make a Buck, One Street Lit Book at a Time." *NPR: Author Interviews*, October 12. www.npr.org/2023/10/12/1204833258/quan-millz-is-out-to-make-a-buck-one-street-lit-book-at-a-time.

Worth, Robert R. 2002. "Claude Brown, Manchild of the Promised Land, Dies at 64." *New York Times*, February 6. www.nytimes.com/2002/02/06/books/claude-brown-manchild-of-the-promised-land-dies-at-64.html.

Wright, Richard. 1940. *Native Son*. New York: Harper and Brothers.

Zanal Abidin, Nur Syazwanie, Norshila Shaifuddin, and Wan Satirah Wan Mohd Saman. 2023. "Systematic Literature Review of the Bibliotherapy Practices in Public Libraries in Supporting Communities' Mental Health and Wellbeing." *Public Library Quarterly* 42, no. 2: 124–40. https://doi.org/10.1080/01616846.2021.2009291.

Zernike, Kate. 2004. "Oh, to Write a 'Bridget Jones' for Men: A Guy Can Dream." *New York Times*, February 22. www.nytimes.com/2004/02/22/style/oh-to-write-a-bridget-jones-for-men-a-guy-can-dream.html.

Zimmer, Melanie. 2002. "Common Symbols of Transformation in Fairy Lore, Legend, and Biblical Stories." Storyteller.net. www.storyteller.net/articles/68 (web page discontinued).

INDEX

A

The Absolute Truth (Williams), 43
Abdul, A., 39–40
active reading, 98–100
Addicted (Zane), xvi
addiction rehabilitation clients, 40
African American literature
  librarian familiarity with, 101
  street lit along historical
    continuum, 75–76
African American Vernacular
  English (AAVE), 22, 71
African Americans
  Christian teen-friendly series,
    46–47
  diversity of street lit, 30
  language of street lit, 22
  nonfiction/fiction along
    historical continuum, 75–76
  street lit during Harlem
    Renaissance, 3–4
  street lit for tweens, 43–47
  street lit, historical continuum
    of, 6–8
  See also Black Americans
Agosto, D. E., 41
Aiex, Nola Kortner, 40
ALA (American Library
  Association), 40
ALA Reader's Advisory series,
  vii–viii
Alessio, Amy, 83
All Hail the Queen: An Urban Tale
  (Mink), 53
All Shot Up (Himes), 10
All the Wrong Moves (Carter), 45
Allen, Debbie, 23

*Always Outnumbered, Always
  Outgunned* (Mosley), 10
Amanda's Ray (Wilke), 48
Amazon.com
  review of street lit by readers,
    20–21, 100
  review of *Thug Lovin'* on,
    36, 99
  for street-lit reviews, 66, 72
  street-lit titles on, 8, 83
American Dream
  living in poverty in America
    vs., 40
  low-income Americans and, 96
  street lit and, 29
American Gangster (film), 58
American Library Association
  (ALA), 40
analysis
  of street lit by readers, 98–100
  value of teens reading street lit,
    50–51
Anderson, Elijah
  *Code of the Street: Decency,
    Violence and the Moral Life of
    the Inner City*, 55, 74
  nonfiction works by, 9
  on obstacles for teens, 41
Andrews, V. C., xvi
Animal (K'wan)
  as beginning of five-volume
    series, 70
  matching books to films, 58
  in readers' advisory display, 57
  as street-lit classic, 68
Anthony, Mark, 71

129

Index

Antoinette, Ashley
See Coleman, Ashley Antoinette
appeal, vii
Appleyard, J. A., 50
Around the Way Girls (Hunter, Hunt, & Joseph), 70
Artemis, Black, 8
Asante, M. K., 56, 74
Ashley
See Coleman, Ashley Antoinette
Asian Americans, 30
Ault, P. B., xiv
authenticity, 54–56
authors
active author, 93–95
ALA Reader's Advisory series on, viii
author book signings, 88, 89
author panel, 89–90
author-reader connection, 95
in conversation with reader/librarian, 93
street-fiction collections, attributes of reputable, 71–72
street-lit authors as literary bards, 105–106
value of teens reading street lit, 50
The Autobiography of Malcolm X (Malcolm X as told to Alex Haley)
old/new street lit, combining, 79
readers' advisory suggestion for, 54
realism/naturalism in, 76
as street lit, 4, 5

B

Badu, Erykah, 82
Baker, Soren, 56
Baker, T. N., 88
Balaji, Murali, 13
Barnes & Noble, 72
Bartlett, Lesley, 102

Barton, David, 41
b-boying, 105
The Beautiful Struggle (Coates), 56
Beck, Robert
See Slim, Iceberg (Robert Beck)
Bentley Manor Tales series (Mink & Diamond), 14–15
Best Kept Secret (Williams), 43
Beta Gamma Pi series (Perry-Moore), 46
Betts, R. Dwayne, 74
Between the World and Me (Coates), 55
bibliotherapy, 40
Billingsley, ReShonda Tate, 46
biographies
list of recommended biographies for collection, 73–74
list of titles, 55–56
titles for foundational street-lit collection, 117–118
Bitch series (King), 70
Bitch: The Beginning (King), 68
Bitch The Final Chapter (King), 70
Black: A Street Tale (Brown)
format of, 22
matching books to films, 58
as street-lit classic, 68
themes of, 18
Black Americans
hip-hop culture, emergence of, xiii–xiv
nonfiction/fiction along historical continuum, 75–76
street literature, canonical agency of, xiii–xx
See also African Americans
Black Boy (Wright), xiv–xv
Black Girl Lost (Goines), ix–x
Blaxploitation film era, 7
Bleeding Violet (Reeves), 48
Blinded (Williams), 43
Blood Relation (Konigsberg), 57

130

Blow (film), 58
Blue, Treasure E.
    as established street-lit author,
        71
    Harlem Girl Lost: A Novel, 68
    Keyshia and Clyde: A Novel, 57
*Blue Rage, Black Redemption: A
    Memoir* (Williams), 56
Bluford High series (Langan)
    appeal of, 24
    description of, 45
    for tweens, 43
BMF: Starz Series (television series),
    58
*BMF: The Rise and Fall of Big
    Meech and the Black Mafia Family*
    (Shalhoup), 57
B-More Careful (Holmes), 25, 68
Bodega Dreams (Quiñonez), 54, 68
Bolnick, Jamie Pastor, 56, 73
Bonanno, Rosalie, 57
book clubs
    book discussions/activities,
        83–86
    field trips for, 88–90
    for librarians, 86–88
    for processing fictional/lived
        stories, 85–86
    self-esteem activities, 84–85
    for street-lit programming, 81,
        82–83
    writing poetry/journaling, 84
*Book Clubs: Women and the Uses of
    Reading in Everyday Life* (Long), 49
book covers
    of street lit for tweens, 43, 45
    of street-lit novels, 24–25
book displays
    guidance on, 82
    for street-lit programming, 81
book festivals/fairs, 88–89
book publishing
    See publishing
Book Review Digest, 72

book reviews
    See reviews
book titles, 25–26
booklist
    contemporary collection, 111–113
    LGBTQIA titles, 113–114
    nonfiction (biographies/
        memoirs), 117–118
    nonfiction (poetry), 116–117
    of street-lit genre, xix
    twentieth-century classics,
        109–110
    twenty-first-century classics,
        110–111
    young adult fiction, 114–115
    young adult series, 115–116
Booklist, 60
books
    banning, 105
    book discussions/activities,
        83–86
    matching books to films for
        readers' advisory display, 58
booktalking, 82
Booth, Coe, 47
Bottigheimer, Ruth B., 16
Bourgois, Phillippe
    Righteous Dopefiend, 74
    *In Search of Respect: Selling Crack
        in El Barrio*, 55, 74
*The Boy Is Mine: A Wilson High
    Confidential* (White), 49
Boyd, K. C., 67
Boyz n the Hood (film), 7
break dancing, xiii–xiv
The Bridge (Jones), 18
Bridget Jones's Diary (Fielding), 28
Britt, A. C., 33
broadsides, 1–2
Brontë, Charlotte, 57, 79, 97
Brooks, Wanda
    on reader comments on street
        lit, 83, 100
    street lit, popularity of, xviii

Index

Brothers of the Knight (Allen), 23
Brown, Claude
  historical continuum of street
    lit, 7
  Manchild in the Promised Land,
    ix, 4–5, 54, 76
Brown, Jericho, 75
Brown, Laurinda D., 33
Brown, Tracy
  Black: A Street Tale, 18, 22, 58, 68
  White Lines: A Novel, 15
Brown Girl, Brownstones (Marshall),
  54
Brown Girl in the Ring (Hopkinson),
  53
Bruner, Jerome, 98
Buck: A Memoir (Asante), 56, 74
Buckhanon, Kalisha, 22, 23
*Bum Rush the Page: A Def Poetry
  Slam* (Medina & Rivera), 75
Burke, Kenneth, 49
Burns, Edward, 55
Butler, Octavia, 18, 53
Butler, Robert, xiv
Buvala, K. Sean, 16

C

Cahan, Abraham, 3, 75
Call It Sleep (Roth), xiv
Campbell, Donna M., 3, 18–19
Canada, Geoffrey, 9, 74
Cannon, Peter, 40
canonical works
  American Dream and, 96
  matching street-lit novels with,
    56, 57
  See also street-lit classics
The Canterbury Tales (Chaucer), 13
capitalistic society, 96
Caramanica, Jon, xviii
Caribbean Americans, 30
Carl Weber's Kingpins: Philadelphia
  (Williams), 58
Carlson, Lori Marie, 9

Carlson, Melody, 47
Carmen Browne series (Perry-
  Moore), 46
The Cartel (Ashley & JaQuavis)
  film pairing with, 58
  music pairing with, 82
  on *New York Times* Best Sellers
    list, 90
  as street-lit classic, 68
  in street-lit fiction series, 70
Cartel Queen: Aries Manifesto
  (Ashley & JaQuavis), 70
Carter, Nikki, 45
Carter, Quentin
  Hoodwinked, 25–26
  setting of stories by, 52
Cash Money Content, 106
censorship
  of books, 105
  sexual content in street lit and,
    66–67
  street-lit book review resources,
    60
Chance, Rosemary, 41
chapbooks, 1–2
characters
  in men's stories/women's
    stories, 31–32
  "the street" as motif, 12–16
  in thug fiction, 34–36
Chaucer, Geoffrey, 13
check-in, 87
chica lit, 29
Chicago Public Library, 64, 65
chick lit
  librarian familiarity with, 101
  subgenres of, 29
  as urban fiction subgenre, 28
Children of the Ghetto (Zangwill), 3
Chiles, Nick, 13
Christian teen-friendly series, 46–47
Christmas holiday reading, 58
*Chronicles of the Juice Man: A
  Memoir* (Juicy J & Baker), 56

132

Index

Chunichi
    See Knott, Chunichi
circulation
    book displays and, 82
    readers' advisory display and, 59–60
    of street-lit titles, strategies for, 76–77
    trends for street lit, 63–66
city novels
    diversity of street lit, 30
    urban fiction, 12
    See also street literature (street lit)
Cityblock (Franceschelli), 23
Civil Rights Act, xiii
Civil Rights Era
    hip-hop culture and, xiii
    historical continuum of street lit, 7
    street literature about, 4–5
    street-lit fiction/nonfiction in, 76
Clark, Wahida
    current-day fictional works by women, 9
    as established street-lit author, 71
    thug fiction of, 34–36, 53
    Thug Lovin', 5, 21–22, 99
    Thug series, 70
    Thugs and the Women Who Love Them, 20–21, 42, 68
    Wahida Clark Presents Young Adult YA imprint, 48–49
    Wahida Clark Publishing, 8
classic titles
    See street-lit classics
Cleopatra Jones (film), 7
Close to Death: Poems (Smith), 75
cluster collection, portable, 78, 79
Coates, Ta-Nehisi
    The Beautiful Struggle, 56
    Between the World and Me, 55

Cochran-Smith, Marilyn, 88
Code of Ethics (American Library Association), 40
Code of the Street: Decency, Violence, and the Moral Life of the Inner City (Anderson), 55, 74
The Coldest Winter Ever (Souljah)
    book cover of, 24
    circulation trends for street-lit titles, 63, 64, 65–66
    in historical continuum of street lit, 5
    librarians and, xvi
    on *New York Times* Best Sellers list, 90
    old/new street lit, combining, 79
    reader completion of, 19
    in readers' advisory display, 57
    reference interview/RA interaction, xvii–xviii
    relationships in, 37
    rise/fall of Winter Santiaga, 16
    as street-lit classic, 68, 69
    street-lit fiction series, 70
    teen readers of, 42
    title of, 25
    Winter's character in, 31
Coleman, Ashley Antoinette
    The Cartel, 58, 68
    as established street-lit author, 71
    Ethic, 26, 99–100
    Moth to a Flame, 57, 68
    novels for addiction rehabilitation clients, 40
    street-lit fiction series, 70
Coleman, JaQuavis
    The Cartel, 58, 68
    novels for addiction rehabilitation clients, 40
    street-fiction collections, established writers, 71
    street-lit fiction series, 70
collaborative writing, 84

Index

collection development
  circulate street-lit collection on seven-day loan, 77
  interfile street fiction, 77
  listening to patrons, 79
  maximum number of titles per patron, 76–77
  old/new titles, combining, 79
  portable cluster collection, 78
  strategies, results of, 79–80
  street literature, foundational collection, 109–118
  street-lit classics, 67–70
  street-lit fiction series, 70–71
collection management
  circulation trends, 63–66
  collection development strategies, 76–79
  collection development strategies, results of, 79–80
  nonfiction/fiction along historical continuum, 75–76
  sexual content/censorship, 66–67
  street-fiction collections, attributes of reputable, 71–73
  street-lit classics, 68–70
  street-lit fiction series, 70–71
  street-lit nonfiction, 73–75
The Color Purple (Walker), 13
commitment, 35
community
  collection development and, 80
  literate librarian and, 102
  reading community, 84
  "the streets" as motif, 14
The Complete Brothers Grimm Fairy Tales (Owens), 41
Compton-Lilly, Catherine, 40
confidentiality, 88
Connected to the Plug (Williams), 26
connection, 50–51
consistency, 94–95

contemporary street lit
  connection with naturalism, 18–19
  consideration of, 5–6
  diversity of, 30
  language of, 22
  matching with canonical works, 57, 80
  readers' advisory for teens, 41–42, 54
  titles for foundational street-lit collection, 111–113
  titles of, 25–26
Convict's Candy (Meadows & Poole), 33
Coretta Scott King Award, 44
The Corner: A Year in the Life of an Inner City Neighborhood (Simon & Burns), 55
covers
  book covers of street lit for tweens, 43, 45
  of street-lit novels, 24–25
Crackhouse: Notes from the End of the Line (Williams), 74
Crane, Stephen
  Maggie: A Girl of the Streets, xvi, 2, 10
  Maggie: A Girl of the Streets, as canonical work, 96
  Maggie: A Girl of the Streets as street survival story, 6
  Maggie: A Girl of the Streets, readers' advisory, 54, 57
  nonfiction/fiction along historical continuum, 75
  self-publishing by, 6
Crews, Nina, 23
critical analysis, 98–100
cross-branch visits, 89
Cruz, José, 4

D

Dad lit, 29
Daddy Cool (Goines), 86

Dafina (publisher), 72
Damaged (Dupree), 30
Dash, Leon, 74
Davis, Sampson, 55
de Leon, Aya, 24
The Dead Emcee Scrolls: The Lost Teachings of Hip-Hop (Williams), 75
Declaration of Independence, x
A Deeper Love Inside: The Porsche Santiaga Story (Souljah), 70
Defoe, Daniel
    Moll Flanders, xvi, 3, 57
    Moll Flanders, rise/fall of character, 16
    Moll Flanders, story of, 6
Denim Diaries series (Lee), 44–45
Desi chick lit, 29
Desperate Hoodwives (Diamond & Bryant), 30
Diamond, De'nesha, 14–15
Diary of a Teenage Girl series (Carlson), 47
Dickens, Charles
    aristocracy's reading of, 1
    Oliver Twist, 3, 6, 16
    Oliver Twist, readers' advisory suggestion for, 54
    Oliver Twist, relationships in, 37
    street-literature novels of, 2
Dickey, Eric Jerome, 28–29
Dimitriadis, George, 41
Dirty Game (Holmes), 5
display
    implications for library circulation, 59–60
    implications of book displays, 58–59
    readers' advisory display, 56–57
Divas series (Murray), 46
diversity
    of street lit, 30
    subgenres of street lit, 29
Divine, L., 23, 44

Divine/Divine Friends series (Thomas), 46
DJ Kool Herc, xiii, 105
DJing
    as element of hip-hop culture, 105
    hip-hop emergence out of, xiii–xiv
DMX, 73, 82
Do the Right Thing (film), 7
documentaries, 74
Donofrio, Beverly, 57
Doom Fox (Iceberg Slim), 76
Dopefiend (Goines), 5, 15–16
Dotson-Lewis, Gloria, 49
double entendres, 25–26
Down These Mean Streets (Thomas), 5, 54
Doyle, Miranda, 96–97
Drama High series (Divine), 23, 44
Draper, Sharon M.
    as established young adult author, 43
    We Beat the Street: How a Friendship Pact Led to Success, 55
Driven (Williams), 43
Dunbar, Paul Laurence
    Skaggs character, 30
    The Sport of the Gods, xiv, 10
    The Sport of the Gods, in readers' advisory display, 57
    The Sport of the Gods, naturalist movement, 75
    The Sport of the Gods, RA suggestion of, 54
Dupree, Kia, 30
Durham (NC) County Library, 64, 65
Dutch II: Angel's Revenge (Woods), 33
Dutch trilogy (Woods & Teague)
    characters in, 8
    Dutch character in, 31–32
    matching with *American Gangster* film, 58

135

Index

Dutch trilogy (Woods & Teague)
(*cont'd*)
   "the street" as character in, 15
   as street-lit classic, 68
   street-lit fiction series, 70
Dymond in the Rough (Williams), 43

E

*E.A.R.L.: The Autobiography of
   DMX* (DMX as told to Smokey D.
   Fontaine), 73
Earth Wind and Fire (band), ix
e-books, 70
Edwards, Mia, 33
Elliott, K., 71
Elliott, Zetta
   genre blending, 18
   A Wish after Midnight, 48, 53
Ellison, Ralph, 57
emceeing, xiii–xiv
Eminem, 86
Endy, 30
entrepreneurialism
   of contemporary street-lit
      authors, 6
   street literature and, x–xi
   of street-lit authors, 69–70
The Equalizer (films), 58
erotica, urban, 36–37
Ervin, Keisha
   Hold U Down, 25–26
   setting of stories by, 52
Essence magazine, 34, 65, 69
Ethic series (Coleman), 26, 99–100
ethnographies
   nonfiction street-lit
      ethnographies, 55
   socio-anthropological
      ethnographies for street-lit
      nonfiction collection, 74
European migration, street lit on,
   3–4
Evans, S. A., 39–40
Every Thug Needs a Lady (Clark), 34

Ex, Kris, 73
expert reader, 96–100
Explicit Content (Artemis), 8

F

Fab Life series (Carter), 45
Fabolous, 82
fairy tales, 16–17
The Family Business (Weber et al.),
   57, 68
family respect, 32
female characters, 31
Ferriss, Susanne, 28
fiction
   interfiling street fiction titles, 77
   readers' advisory display, 57
   street-lit works, 9–10
   street literature, history of,
      9–10
   street-fiction collections,
      attributes of reputable, 71–73
   street-lit fiction series, 70–71
   See also street literature,
      foundational collection
field trips
   best practices, 89–90
   for street-lit programming, 81
   for street-lit book clubbers,
      88–89
Fielding, Helen, 28
50 Cent, 73
films
   matching books to films, 58
   street-lit historical continuum
      and, 7
*Fist Stick Knife Gun: A Personal
   History of Violence* (Canada), 74
Fitzgerald, F. Scott, 96
Flake, Sharon G.
   as established young adult
      author, 43, 44
   street-lit titles for young adults,
      23
Flowers in the Attic (Andrews), xvi

Index

Flyy Girl (Tyree)
old/new street lit, combining, 79
as street-lit classic, 68, 69
Fontaine, Smokey D., 73
For Colored Girls Who Have Considered Suicide/When the Rainbow Is Enuf (Shange), xv
"For the Money" (Fabolous & Nicki Minaj), 82
formats
multiple, 106
of street lit, 22–24, 66
The Fortunate Pilgrim (Puzo), 3, 6
Foye, K'wan
Animal, 57, 58
author visits/events, 88
Hood Rat, 10
Hoodlum: A Novel, 10
impact of books by, 69
librarians and street lit, xvi
novels for addiction rehabilitation clients, 40
old/new street lit, combining, 79
Road Dawgz, 82
Section 8, 30, 31, 32, 42
setting of stories by, 52
street-fiction collections, established writers, 72
street-lit classics by, 68
street-lit fiction series, 70
Franceschelli, Christopher, 23
Free Library of Philadelphia
circulation trends for street-lit titles, 64, 65
Irvin's reference interview/RA interaction, xvii–xviii
Frisby, Mister Mann, 33
From Pieces to Weight: Once Upon a Time in Southside Queens (50 Cent with Kris Ex), 73
Frost, Helen, 9
FUBU (For Us, By Us) apparel line, xi

G

Gang Leader for a Day: A Rogue Sociologist Takes to the Streets (Venkatesh), 55, 74
Gangsta (K'wan), 68
A Gangster's Girl series (Chunichi), 7–8
Gates, Henry Louis, 25
gender
diversity in street-lit genre, 30
men's stories/women's stories, 31–32
of nonfiction/fiction street-lit authors, 9
genres
ALA Reader's Advisory series on, viii
readers' advisory questions about story, 53
subgenres of street lit, 28–29
ghetto, 1–2
ghetto lit, 12
ghetto pulp-fiction novels, 7
Gibson, Simone, 9, 41
Gifford, Justin, xiv
Girls from da Hood (Turner & Hernandez), 70
The Godfather (Puzo), xiv, 96
Goggles! (Keats), 23, 86
Goines, Donald
Black Girl Lost, ix–x
Daddy Cool, 86
Dopefiend, 5, 15–16
first street-lit novels, 105
nonfiction/fiction along historical continuum, 76
novels for addiction rehabilitation clients, 40
realistic portraits of street life, 7
Good Girlz series (Billingsley), 46
Goodreads
reader reviews from, 66, 99–100
as street-lit book review resource, 60

Gorman, Michele Elizabeth, 41, 83
Gossip Girl series (Ziegesar), 28
Graaff, Kristina, 13
Grace after Midnight: A Memoir (Pearson & Ritz), 56, 73
graffiti, xiv, 105
Grand Central Publishing, 72
Grand Central Winter: A Portrait of Chicago and American Segregation (Moore), 74
Grandmaster Flash and the Furious Five, x
Gray, Erick S., 72
The Great Gatsby (Fitzgerald), 96
Great Migration
    nonfiction/fiction along historical continuum, 75
    street lit on, 3–4
Griffin, E. L., 72
Grimey (Williams), 25–26, 43
The Grio Daily, ix
Guerra, Stephanie F., 40
Guidelines for Behavioral Performance of Reference and Information Service Providers (RUSA), 40

H
Hakutani, Yoshinobu, xiv
Haley, Alex, 4, 5, 54, 76, 79
Hamilton, Mary, 41
Hansberry, Lorraine, xv
Harlem Book Fair, 89
Harlem Girl Lost: A Novel (Blue), 68
Harlem Renaissance, 3–4
Harriot, Michael, ix
The Hate U Give (Thomas), 46
Hawthorne, Tash, 30
Haywood, Antoine, 25
Hernandez, Treasure
    The Family Business, 57
    street-fiction collections, established writers, 72

Himes, Chester
    All Shot Up, 10
    historical continuum of street lit, 7
    nonfiction/fiction along historical continuum, 75
    The Real Cool Killers, 79
hip-hop
    birth of, ix
    entrepreneurialism in, x, x–xi
    hip-hop lit, 11, 12
    history of, xiii–xiv
    Old School/New School music, ix
    street lit emergence and, 7
    street lit, popularity of, xviii
    street lit's connection to, 105–106
    street literature and, xv
    "the streets" as powerful symbol, 13
    value of teens reading street lit, 49
historical continuum
    nonfiction/fiction along, 75–76
    relationships in street-lit stories, 37
    of street lit, 6–8
The HistoryMakers, xi
Hold U Down (Ervin), 25–26
Holland, Dorothy, 102
Hollywood High (Simone), 45
Holmes, Shannon
    B-More Careful, 25, 68
    Dirty Game, 5
    Never Go Home Again, 95
    old/new street lit, combining, 79
Holter, Jessica, 75, 76
Homer, 13
Homo Thug (Kahari), 32
"the hood"
    "the street" as motif, 15–16
    "the streets" as synonymous with, 14
    use of term, 12

Index

Hood Rat (K'wan), 10
Hoodlum: A Novel (K'wan), 10
Hoodwinked (Carter), 25–26
Hopkinson, Nalo, 53
Hornby, Nick, 29
"How Bigger Was Born" (Wright), 4
"How I Got Over" (song by The
  Roots), 82
Howe, Irving, 5
Hua, Anh, 50
Hughes, Rashawn, 48–49
Hughes brothers, 7
Hunt, La Jill, 57
Hunt, Rameck, 55
Hustlers (film), 58
A Hustler's Wife (Turner)
  as street-lit classic, 68, 69
  as street-lit fiction series, 70
Hyman, Paula Chase, 47

I

*I Choose to Stay: A Black Teacher
  Refuses to Desert the Inner City*
  (Thomas-El with Murphey), 73
Ice (Robbins)
  conquering the streets in, 16
  males in, 32
  readers' advisory display, 57
Ice-T, 76
identity formation, 18
imagination, 97–98
immigrants
  diversity of street lit, 30
  migration/survival, street lit
    on, 3–4
In My Hood (Endy), 30
In My Skin (Eminem), 86
*In Search of Respect: Selling Crack in
  El Barrio* (Bourgois), 55, 74
inclusivity, 101
indeterminate gap, 97–98
India, 58
interpretation, 11
Interscope Records, xi

Invisible Man (Ellison), 57
Iovine, Jimmy, xi
Irish immigrants, 3
Irvin, Vanessa
  advocacy for street lit, xx
  on authors, 93
  Kafi D. Kumasi on writing of,
    ix–xi
  on library censorship of street
    lit, 67
  on perspective from reading
    street lit, 96–97
  on readers of street lit, 11
  reference interview/RA
    interaction, xvii–xviii
  on "the street" as silent
    antagonist, 14
  street lit, popularity of, xviii
  street-lit genre elements debate,
    13
  on teen readers of street lit, 40,
    41
  on time taken to read street-lit
    novel, 76–77
  on value of teens reading street
    lit, 49
Isay, David, 55, 74
Iser, Wolfgang
  on impact of reading, 98
  on indeterminate gap, 98
  "movie in the head" idea, 19
  on reader response theory,
    xvii
  on teen readers of street lit, 97
  value of teens reading street
    lit, 50
Italian immigrants, 3

J

Jackson, Renay, 52
Jane Eyre (Brontë)
  matching with *Wifey* (Swinson),
    57
  teen reading of, 79, 97

Index

JaQuavis
   See Coleman, JaQuavis
Jason's Lyric (film), 58
Jayden's Impossible Garden
   (Mangal), 23
Jenkins, George, 55
Jenkins, Jerry B., 47
Jewish immigrants, 3
John, Daymond, xi
Johnson, Angela, 43
Jones, Charisse, 4
Jones, Gerald Everett, 28
Jones, LeAlan, 55, 74
Jones, Solomon
   The Bridge, 18
   Ride or Die, 53
   setting of stories by, 52
journaling, 84
Juicy J, 56
Justify My Thug (Clark), 34

K

Kahari, Asante, 32
Karma with a Vengeance
   (Hawthorne), 30
Karrington, Blake, 72
Keats, Ezra Jack, 23, 86
Keesha's House (Frost), 9
Kensington Books, 20
Keyshia and Clyde: A Novel (Blue),
   57
keywords, 51–52
Kimani Tru series (Various
   Authors), 45
King, Joy Deja
   Bitch series, 70
   Bitch: The Beginning, 68
   circulation trends for street-lit
      titles, 64, 65–66
   Stackin' Paper, 82
   street-fiction collections,
      established writers, 72
Kingpins series (Weber), 70
Kirkus Reviews, 60, 72

Kiss the Girls and Make Them Cry
   (Williams), 58
Knott, Chunichi
   A Gangster's Girl series, 7–8
   old/new street lit, combining,
      79
   street-fiction collections,
      established writers, 71
knowledge, 105
Konigsberg, Eric, 57
Kotlowitz, Alex, 9
Kumasi, Kafi D., ix–xi, 41
K'wan
   See Foye, K'wan

L

lad lit
   librarian familiarity with, 101
   as urban fiction subgenre,
      28–29
*Lady Q: The Rise and Fall of a Latin
   Queen* (Sanchez & Rodriguez),
   56, 74
LaHaye, Tim, 47
Landay, Eileen, 95
Langan, Paul, 24
language
   book titles for street lit, 25–26
   SAE, street-fiction collection
      in, 71
   of street lit, 22
Latino literature, 101
Latinx Americans, 7–8, 30
Lavenne, François-Xavier, 50
LeBlanc, Adrian Nicole, 55, 57, 74
Lee, Darrien, 44–45
Lee, Spike, 7
Left Behind series (LaHaye &
   Jenkins), 47
legacy, of street literature, 105–107
Let That Be the Reason (Stringer)
   author sales of, 6
   publication of, x
   as street-lit classic, 68, 69

Index

LGBTQIA+ literature
  librarian familiarity with, 101
  overview of, 32–34
  in street-lit genre, 30
  titles for foundational street-lit
    collection, 113–114
librarians
  book club meetings facilitated
    by, 83–84
  book clubs for, 86–88
  in conversation with author/
    reader, 93
  literate librarian, 102–103
  promotion of street lit/literacy,
    90–91
  readers' advisory for street lit,
    39–41
  readers' advisory for teens, 41–42
  readers' advisory, stance on, 61
  reading librarian, 100–101
  search terms/keywords for
    street lit, 51–52
  sexual content in street lit and,
    66–67
  street-lit book review resources,
    60
  street lit, reading of, xviii–xix
  street-lit book club, 85
libraries
  circulation trends for street-lit
    titles, 63–66
  street lit offered by, 8
library circulation
  See circulation
Library Journal, 72
Library of Congress (LOC), 51
library programming for street lit
  book clubs, 82–83
  book clubs for librarians, 86–88
  book discussions/activities,
    83–86
  book displays, 82
  field trips, 88–90
  overview of, 81

  promotion of street lit/literacy,
    90–91
life, 13
*Life After Death: The Coldest Winter
  Ever*, Part 2 (Souljah), 68, 70, 99
listening, 80
literacy
  events for street-lit
    programming, 81
  field trips for street-lit readers,
    89
  promoting street lit and, 90–91
literacy practice, reading street
  lit as
  active author, 93–95
  authors/readers/librarians and,
    93
  expert reader, 96–100
  literate librarian, 102–103
  reading librarian, 100–101
Little, Terra, 17, 32
*Living at the Edge of the World: A
  Teenager's Survival in the Tunnels
  of Grand Central Station* (Tina S. &
  Bolnick), 56, 73
loan period, 77
LOC (Library of Congress), 51
location, 52
London Reign (Britt), 33
Long, Elizabeth, 49
Long Live the Cartel (Ashley &
  JaQuavis), 70
Los Angeles Public Library, 64, 65
Love Lockdown (Edwards), 33
Love Monkey (Smith), 28
lower-income city neighborhoods
  characteristics of street lit, 17–19
  format of street lit, 22–24
  street-lit setting, 29
  street lit *vs.* urban erotica, 36–37
Luther: BBC Series, 58
Luu, Chi, 25
Lytle, Susan L., 88
Lyubymova, Svitlana, 40

141

M

Mabry, Celia Hales, 102
Mafia Marriage: My Story (Bonanno & Donofrio), 57
Maggie: A Girl of the Streets (Crane)
  as canonical work, 10, 96
  in historical continuum of street lit, 6
  librarians and, xvi
  publication story of, 2
  in readers' advisory display, 57
  readers' advisory suggestion for, 54
  self-publishing of, 6
  as street literature, 2
Makes Me Wanna Holler: A Young Black Man in America (McCall)
  demand for, 5
  RA recommendation of, 55
  for street-lit nonfiction collection, 73
Malcolm X
  The Autobiography of Malcolm X, 4, 5, 54, 76
  historical continuum of street lit, 7
  old/new street lit, combining, 79
male characters, 31–32
Mama Black Widow: A Story of the South's Black Underworld (Iceberg Slim), 5
Manchild in the Promised Land (Brown)
  in Civil Rights Era, 76
  as old school street lit, ix–x
  readers' advisory suggestion for, 54
  as street lit, 4–5
Mangal, Mélina, 23
The Manny (Peterson), 28
Marcou, D., 19
marketing, viii, 81
Marshall, Elizabeth, 9
Marshall, Paule, 54

Martin, Philip, 3
Master P (rapper), xi
McCall, Nathan, 5, 55, 73
McDonald, Janet
  as established young adult author, 43
  Project Girl, 23, 55, 57, 73
McFadden, Bernice L., 13
MCing, 105
McKayhan, Monica, 45
McTeague (Norris), 3
Meadows, Damon Amin, 33
Medina, Tony, 75
memoirs
  list of recommended biographies for collection, 73–74
  list of titles, 55–56
  titles for foundational street-lit collection, 117–118
Menace II Society (film), 7
men's stories, 30, 31–32
Meow Meow Productions, x
Merriam-Webster's online dictionary, 27–28
Michael L. Printz Award, 44
Midnight: A Gangster Love Story (Souljah), 22, 24
Midnight and the Meaning of Love (Souljah), 24
Midnight trilogy (Souljah)
  circulation trends for, 66
  diversity of city neighborhoods in, 30
  matching books to films for readers' advisory display, 58
  publication of, 70
migration, 3–4
Millington, Mil, 28
Minaj, Nicki, 82
Mind of My Mind (Butler), 18, 53
Mink, Meesha, 14–15, 53
Moll Flanders (Defoe)
  librarians and, xvi

Index

matching street-lit novel with, 57
rise/fall of character in streets, 16
story of, 3, 6
The Moments, the Minutes, the Hours: The Poetry of Jill Scott (Scott), 9, 75
Monique, Asia, 57
Monster (Myers), 44, 57
Monster: The Autobiography of an L. A. Gang Member (Shakur)
   demand for, 5
   RA recommendation of, 55
   in readers' advisory display, 57
Moore, Natalie Y., 74
Moore, Wes, 74
Morris, DeShaun "Jiwe," 74
Morris, Vanessa
   See Irvin, Vanessa
Mosley, Walter, 10
Moth to a Flame (Antoinette), 57, 68
"movie in the head" idea, 19–20
movies
   Blaxploitation film era, 7
   field trips to, 88
   matching street-lit titles with, 56, 58
multiple-title approach, 83
Murphey, Cecil, 73
Murray, Victoria Christopher, x, 46
music
   hip-hop, x–xi, xiii
   Old School music, ix
   street lit emergence and, 7
   street lit/music pairings, 82
   street lit's legacy, 105
   teens reading street lit and, 49
My Bloody Life: The Making of a Latin King (Sanchez), 55, 73
My Feet Are Laughing (Norman), 23
My Secrets Your Lies (N'Tyse), 34
Myers, Walter Dean
   as established young adult author, 43, 44

Monster, in readers' advisory display, 57
   street-lit titles for young adults, 23
Street Love, 9, 75
mystery, 53

N

National Linguistic University, Kyiv, Ukraine, 40
Native Son (Wright)
   Hoodlum: A Novel (K'wan) and, 10
   readers' advisory suggestion for, 54
   as street lit, 3–4
   Vanessa Irvin and, xiv–xv
naturalism
   nonfiction/fiction along historical continuum, 75–76
   street lit's connection to, 18
   of street-lit classics, 69
   works that sparked, 3
The Neighborhood Mother Goose (Crews), 23
Nero, Clarence, 33
Never Go Home Again (Holmes), 95
New School, ix
New York Times, 72
New York Times Best Sellers list
   Every Thug Needs a Lady (Clark) on, 34
   street-lit titles on, 69, 76, 90
   Wahida Clark's book on, 21
Newman, Katherine S., 9
Newman, Lloyd, 55, 74
Nicholas, James, 74
Nilsen, Kirsti, 102
Ninety-Nine Problems (Dotson-Lewis), 49
Ni-Ni Girl Chronicles (Simone), 45
Nishikawa, Kinohi, 13
Nix, Taylor, 90
No Limit Records, xi

Index

nonfiction
  along historical continuum,
    75–76
  biographies or memoirs, 73–74
  diversity of street lit, 30
  interfiling street fiction titles, 77
  poetry, 75, 116–117
  readers' advisory display, 57
  readers' advisory questions,
    54–56
  as significant aspect of street-lit
    genre, 5
  socio-anthropological
    ethnographies, 74
  street lit works, 9–10
  street literature, history of, 9–10
  street-lit nonfiction, 73–75
  titles for foundational street-lit
    collection, 116–118
Norman, Lissette, 23
Norris, Frank, 3
Not a Good Look (Carter), 45
NoveList, 60, 66
novels
  broadsides, metamorphosis
    into, 2
  migration/survival, street lit
    on, 3–4
  See also fiction; street literature
    (street lit)
N'Tyse, 34

O

The Odyssey (Homer), 13
Old School literature, ix–x
Oliver Twist (Dickens)
  readers' advisory questions, 54
  relationships in, 37
  rise/fall of character in streets,
    16
  story of, 3, 6
  in street-literature history, 1
online public access catalog
  (OPAC), 51–52

The Other Wes Moore: One Name,
  Two Fates (Moore), 74
"Otherside of the Game" (song by
  Erykah Badu), 82
Our America: Life and Death on the
  South Side of Chicago (Jones &
  Newman with Isay), 55, 74
Overbrook Park Branch Library,
  Philadelphia, 43
Owens, Lily, 41

P

patrons
  book clubs for street lit, 82–83
  book discussions/activities,
    83–86
  listening to, 79
  readers' advisory display and,
    59–60
  readers' advisory for street lit,
    39–41
  readers' advisory questions,
    52–56
  street-lit book review resources,
    60
  street-lit programming for, 81–91
  See also readers
Payton Skyy series (Perry-Moore),
  46
Pearson, Felicia "Snoop," 56, 73
Pernice, Ronda Racha, 13
Perry Skyy, Jr. series (Perry-Moore),
  46
Perry-Moore, Stephanie, 46
perspective, 96–98
Pete, Eric, 57, 68
Peterson, Holly, 28
Petry, Ann
  historical continuum of street
    lit, 6, 75
  The Street, xv, 3–4, 15, 54, 79
Pettegree, Andrew, 1
Philadelphia Free Library Book
  Festival, 89–90

Index

Philadelphia Librarian Book Club, 19–20
Phillips, C. N., 57, 72
picture books, 23
Pimp: The Story of My Life (Iceberg Slim), 5
Platinum Persuasion (India), 58
Platinum Teen trilogy (Williams)
  publication of, 23, 43
  as vital to YA literature, 44
Please (Brown), 75
poetry
  as book club activity, 84
  street-lit poetry, 9
  for street-lit nonfiction collection, 75
  titles for foundational street-lit collection, 116–117
polling, 87
Poole, Jason, 33
portable cluster collection, 78, 79
poverty
  characteristics of street lit, 17
  in ghetto, 12
  reader awareness of, 56
  relationships and, 37
  in street lit, 20, 29, 40–41
  thug fiction on, 35
  as urban fiction theme, 36–37
Precious: Based on the Novel Push by Sapphire (film), 66
Precioustymes Entertainment Publishing company, 43
professional development, 86–88
programming
  See library programming for street lit
A Project Chick (Turner), 57
Project Girl (McDonald)
  RA recommendation of, 55
  in readers' advisory display, 57
  story of, 23
  for street-lit nonfiction collection, 73

promotion
  library programming for street lit, 81
  of street lit/literacy, 90–91
protagonist triad, 16, 17
Public Enemy #1 (Swinson), 53
publishers
  rejection of street lit, 6
  of street fiction, established, 72
  of street lit, 20
  of street lit for tweens, 43
  of street lit, rapid change in, 106
Publishers Weekly, 60, 72
publishing
  publishers of color, x–xi
  self-publishing by street-lit authors, 8
  self-publishing of teen-friendly street lit, 44
Push (Relentless Aaron), 68
Push (Sapphire)
  circulation trends for, 64, 65–66
  double-entendre title of, 25–26
  mentor in, 17
  as street-lit classic, 68
Puzo, Mario
  The Fortunate Pilgrim, 3
  The Godfather, xiv, 96
  historical continuum of street lit, 6, 75

Q

Queen Bitch series, Part 4 (King), 64, 65–66
A Question of Freedom: A Memoir of Learning, Survival, and Coming of Age in Prison (Betts), 74
questions, for readers' advisory, 52–56
Quiñonez, Ernesto, 54, 68
Quitana, I., 51

Index

R

Racheal, Christine, 33–34
Radford, Marie L., 102
Radway, Janice, 18
Rafferty, Terrence, 18
A Raisin in the Sun (Hansberry), xv
Random Family: Love, Drugs, Trouble, and Coming of Age in the Bronx (LeBlanc)
  in readers' advisory display, 57
  for street-lit nonfiction collection, 55, 74
Ranganathan, S. R., 102
reaction sheets, 86–87
read-alikes, viii
reader response theory, xvi–xvii
readers
  active reading, self-reflection, analysis, 98–100
  author, relationship with, 93–95
  book clubs for street lit, 82–83
  characteristics of street lit and, 19
  in conversation with author/ librarian, 93
  enjoyment of street lit, 11
  legacy of street lit, 105–107
  listening to, 79, 85
  online reviews for collection management, 66
  perspective from reading street lit, 96–98
  promoting street lit/literacy, 90–91
  readers' advisory for street lit, 39–41
  readers' advisory questions, 52–56
  reading librarian and, 101
  reality reflected in street lit, 19–20
  street lit as "movie in the head," 19–20
  street-lit programming for, 81

  street-lit stories for, 96
  street-lit structural elements and, 20–22
  See also patrons
readers' advisory (RA)
  ALA Reader's Advisory series for, vii–viii
  display, 56–60
  librarian as lifelong learner, 102
  librarian's stance on, 61
  overview of, 39–41
  questions for, 52–56
  search terms/keywords for street lit, 51–52
  for street literature, xvi–xx
  for teens, 41–42
  teens reading street lit, value of, 49–51
  for tweens, 43–47
  young adult titles, 48–49
reading
  active, 98–100
  book clubs for street lit, 82–83
  librarian, 100–101
  promotion of street lit for, 90–91
  value of teens reading street lit, 49–51
Reading Is My Window: Books and the Art of Reading in Women's Prisons (Sweeney), 55
reading street lit as literacy practice
  active author, 93–95
  authors/readers/librarians and, 93
  expert reader, 96–100
  literate librarian, 102–103
  reading librarian, 100–101
Reading the Romance (Radway), 18
The Real Cool Killers (Himes), 79
realism, 69
reality
  author-reader connection and, 95

Index

indeterminate gap and, 97–98
reader analysis of street lit, 100
teen readers of street lit and,
40–41
Red Badge of Courage (Crane), 2
*Red Hot Salsa: Bilingual Poems on
Being Young and Latino in the
United States* (Carlson), 9
Reeves, Dia, 48
Reference and User Services
Association, 40
reflection, 50–51
regional dialects, 22
relationships
poverty and, 37
street-lit characteristics, 18
relativity, 54
Relentless Aaron
old/new street lit, combining, 79
Push, as street-lit classic, 68
sale of books by, 69
setting of stories by, 52
street-fiction collections,
established writers, 71
religion, 46–47
reluctant readers, 81, 91
Renard, Virginie, 50
representation, 11, 101
research narratives, 55
resources
for keeping up to date with
genre or subject, viii
street-lit book review resources,
60
street/urban literature,
foundational collection,
109–118
reviews
credible review sources, 72–73
by readers, 20–22, 99–100
street-lit book review resources,
60
for street-lit collection
management, 66

Richardson, Fox, 56
Richardson, Rob, 56
Ride or Die (Jones), 53
Righteous Dopefiend (Bourgois), 74
Ringgold, Faith, 23
Ritz, David, 56, 73
Rivera, Jeff, 76
Rivera, Louis Reyes, 75
Road Dawgz (K'wan), 82
Robbins, Will
Ice, 16, 32
Ice, in readers' advisory display,
57
Rodriguez, Sonia, 56, 74
rolling book cart, 59
romance
readers' advisory questions, 53
street lit *vs.* urban erotica, 36–37
in thug fiction, 35
The Roots, 82
*Rosa Lee: A Mother and Her Family
in Urban America* (Dash), 74
The Rose That Grew from Concrete
(Shakur), 9, 75
Rosenblatt, Louise M.
"movie in the head" idea, 19
on reader response theory, xvii
value of teens reading street
lit, 50
Ross, Catherine Sheldrick, 102
Roth, Henry, xiv
routine, 94–95
"Ruff Ryders' Anthem" (song by
DMX), 82
Runaway (Williams), 43

S

S., Tina, 56, 73
SAE (Standard American English),
71
Saffou, Mazin Bashire, 40
Sanchez, Reymundo
*Lady Q: The Rise and Fall of a
Latin Queen*, 56, 74

Index

Sanchez, Reymundo (*cont'd*)
   My Bloody Life: The Making of a Latin King, 55, 73
   nonfiction/fiction along historical continuum, 76
Sanchez, Sonia, 75
Sapphire
   circulation trends for street-lit titles, 65–66
   Push, as street-lit classic, 68
   Push, circulation trends for, 64
   Push, double-entendre title of, 25–26
Saricks, Joyce, vii–viii
Savage, Lorraine
   on reader comments on street lit, 83, 100
   street lit, popularity of, xviii
Scholastic Press, 45
school assignment, 54
School Library Journal, 73
Scott, Jill, 9, 75
search terms, 51–52
Section 8: A Hood Rat Novel (K'wan)
   China character in, 30
   librarian respect of teen choices, 42
   Tech character in, 32
   Tionna character in, 31
self, sense of, 50–51
self-esteem activities, 84–85
self-publishing
   by street-lit authors, 8
   of teen-friendly street lit, 44
   by twenty-first century street-lit authors, 6
self-reflection, 98–100
Sendak, Maurice, 23
series, street-lit fiction series, 70–71
setting, 52
Sewell, Earl, 45
sexuality
   LGBTQIA+ stories, 32–34

sexual content in street lit, 66–67
   street-lit book covers and, 24
Shaft (film), 7
Shakur, Sanyika, 5, 55, 57
Shakur, Tupac
   The Rose That Grew from Concrete, 9, 75
   on thug term, 34–35
Shalhoup, Mara, 57
Shange, Ntozake, xv
Shepard, Leslie, 1, 2, 76
Shetani's Sister (Iceberg Slim), 58
Shipler, David K., 9
silent antagonist, 14
Simon, David, 55
Simon & Schuster, 20, 72
Simone, Ni-Ni, 45–46
Sinful Vow: An Arranged Marriage Mafia Romance (Mafia Misfits) (Monique), 57
Singleton, John, 7
Sisselman, Peggy, 102
sistah lit, 29
Sitomer, Alan Lawrence, 47
slang, 22
Slim, Iceberg (Robert Beck)
   chronicling of urban street life, xiv
   first street-lit novels, 105
   nonfiction/fiction along historical continuum, 76
   novels for addiction rehabilitation clients, 40
   realistic portraits of street life, 7
   Shetani's Sister, 58
   titles by, 5
   Vanessa Irvin's reading of, xviii
slum novels
   Maggie: A Girl of the Streets (Crane), 2
   migration/survival street lit, 3–4
   respectable place in libraries, 9–10

street lit's depiction of life in
ghetto, 1–2
Smith, Duncan, 39–40
Smith, Kyle, 28
Smith, Patricia, 75
Smithsonian American Art
Museum, 3
The Snowy Day (Keats), 23, 86
So for Real series (Carter), 45
social media
author engagement with tweens
via, 44, 45–46
book reviews on, 60
reader interaction via, 106
reader responses to street lit on,
20, 21–22
teen literacy on, 85–86
socio-anthropological
ethnographies, 74
sociocultural literacy, 102
Souljah, Sister
book covers of, 24
circulation trends for street-lit
titles, 65–66
The Coldest Winter Ever, xvi,
xvii–xviii, 5, 42
The Coldest Winter Ever,
circulation trends, 64
The Coldest Winter Ever, impact
of, 10
The Coldest Winter Ever, reader
completion of, 19
The Coldest Winter Ever,
relationships in, 37
The Coldest Winter Ever, title of, 25
The Coldest Winter Ever, Winter
character in, 16, 31
current-day fictional works by
women, 9
*Life After Death: A Novel (The
Coldest Winter Ever Book 2)*, 99
matching books to films, 58
Midnight: A Gangster Love Story,
22

Midnight trilogy, 30
nonfiction/fiction along
historical continuum, 76
old/new street lit, combining, 79
readers' advisory display, 57
setting of stories by, 52
street-fiction collections,
established writers, 72
street-lit classics, 68, 69
street-lit fiction, impact on, 63
street-lit fiction series by, 70
Speak the Unspeakable (Holter), 75
speculative fiction, 53
The Sport of the Gods (Dunbar)
as classic, 10
in naturalist movement, 75
in readers' advisory display, 57
readers' advisory suggestion
for, 54
Skaggs character in, 30
Vanessa Irvin and, xiv
St. Martin's Griffin, 72
St. Martin's Press, 20, 69
Stackin' Paper (King), 82
Stallman, Robert Wooster, 2
Standard American English (SAE),
71
Staples, Jeanine, 9
Statista, 12
story, 53
storytelling
"the street" as motif, 12–16
in street lit, 16–17
Strapped (Brown), 33
Strasser, Todd, 47
"the street"
as interactive stage, 17
as motif, 12–16
as transformational force, 16–17
validation of teen readers'
experience, 11
The Street (Petry)
historical continuum of street
lit, 6

Index

"the street" (*cont'd*)
old/new street lit, combining, 79
readers' advisory suggestion for, 54
"the street" as character in, 15
as street lit, 3–4
Vanessa Irvin and, xv
Street Literature: Bringing You the Word on Street Lit and Libraries blog, 14
street literature (street lit)
in British literary tradition, xv
canonical agency of, xiii–xx
circulation trends, 63–66
classifying, 27–29
conservative origins of, x
diversity of, 30
hip-hop and, ix
legacy of, 105–107
LGBTQIA+ stories, 32–34
men's stories/women's stories, 31–32
overview of book's coverage of, xix–xx
reading, as literacy practice, 93–103
subgenres/terminology of, 29
thug fiction, 34–36
urban erotica *vs.*, 36–37
Vanessa Irvin's work with, xiv–xviii
street literature, characteristics of
fairy tales/traditional storytelling, 16–17
introduction to, 11
names for genre, 12
overview of, 17–19
reader's reality reflected in street lit, 19–20
"the street" as motif, 12–16
structural elements, 20–26
street literature, foundational collection

contemporary collection, 111–113
LGBTQIA titles, 113–114
nonfiction (including biographies/memoirs), 117–118
nonfiction (poetry), 116–117
twentieth-century classics, 109–110
twenty-first-century classics, 110–111
young adult series, 115–116
young adult urban fiction, 114–115
street literature, history of
broadsides/chapbooks, 1–2
Civil Rights Movement, 4–5
contemporary street lit, 5–6
development of, 2
fiction/nonfiction, 9–10
historical continuum of street lit, 6–8
migration/survival, 3–4
street literature, library programming for
book clubs, 82–83
book clubs for librarians, 86–88
book discussions/activities, 83–86
book displays, 82
field trips, 88–90
overview of, 81
promotion of street lit/literacy, 90–91
Street Love (Myers), 9, 75
street-lit classics
for booktalk, 78
combining with contemporary titles, 79, 80
for library collection, 67–68
library collection management and, 66
list of titles for collection development, 68–70

Index

twentieth-century classics, 109–110

twenty-first-century classics, 110–111

See also canonical works

street-lit fiction series

introduction to, 68

overview of, 70–71

Stringer, Vickie M.

author visits/events, 88

current-day fictional works by women, 9

as established street-lit author, 72

Let That Be the Reason, 6, 68, 69

Triple Crown Publications, x

structural elements

book covers, 24–25

format, 22–24

language, 22

reader reviews of street lit, 20–22

titles, 25–26

Style, T., 72

subgenres, of street lit, 29

Suellentrop, Tricia Ann, 41, 83

Sumara, Dennis J.

on reading street lit, 97

on street lit/real-life connections, 41

value of teens reading street lit, 50

summer reading programs, 58

Super Fly (film), 7

survival

Civil Rights Era street lit, 4–5

fiction/nonfiction street lit, 9–10

historical continuum of street lit, 6–8

in LGBTQIA+ novels, 34

picture books that depict, 23

street lit characteristics, 18

street literature on, 3–4, 11

in thug definition, 34–35

Sweeney, Megan, 55, 82

Swinson, Kiki

old/new street lit, combining, 79

Public Enemy #1, 53

setting of stories by, 52

Wifey, 42, 57, 79

Wifey, as street-lit classic, 68

Wifey, teen reading of, 97

T

A Tale of Two Cities (Dickens), 1

Tar Beach (Ringgold), 23

Teague, Kwame, 58, 68

teens

book clubs for street lit, 83, 85–86

enjoyment of street lit, 11

field trips for street-lit readers, 88–90

perspective from reading street lit, 97

promotion of street lit/literacy, 90–91

readers' advisory for teens, 41–42

reading street lit, learning from, 94

reading street lit, reasons for, 40–41

reading street lit, value of, 49–51

self-esteem activities, 84–85

street lit as "movie in the head," 19–20

teen-friendly YA titles, 48–49

tweens, street lit for, 43–47

Terraformed: Young Black Lives in the Inner City (White), 55

theft rate, of street fiction, 76–77

themes, 17–19

Thomas, Angie, 46

Thomas, Jacquelin, 46

Thomas, Piri, 5, 54

Index

Thomas-Bailey, Carlene, 24
Thomas-El, Salome, 73
A Thousand and One (film), 58
Three Girls from Bronzeville: A Uniquely American Memoir of Race, Fate, and Sisterhood (Turner), 74
Three Sides to Every Story (Nero), 33
Throwback Diaries (Simone), 45
thug, definition of, 34–35
thug fiction
    for romance readers, 53
    romantic lens of street lit, 36
    of Wahida Clark, 34–36
Thug Lovin' (Clark)
    customer reviews of, 21–22
    in historical continuum of street lit, 5
    on *New York Times* Best Sellers list, 90
    reader post on Amazon.com, 99
    reviews of, 36
Thug Matrimony (Clark), 34
"thug-ism," 35
thug-love fiction, 21
Thugs and the Women Who Love Them (Clark)
    as beginning of *Thug* series, 70
    librarian respect of teen choices, 42
    love in, 35
    reader review of, 20–21
    as street-lit classic, 68
    Wahida Clark's dominance in thug fiction, 34
Thugs: Seven (Clark), 34
Time: The Untold Story of the Love That Held Us Together When Incarceration Kept Us Apart (Richardson & Richardson), 56
titles, book, 25–26
Tollet, François, 50
Training Day (film), 58
transformation, 17

Trick Baby (film), 7
Trickery (Racheal), 33–34
Triple Crown Publications
    book covers of, 24–25
    closure of, 106
    success of, x
True to the Game (Woods)
    author sales of, 6
    as first title of trilogy, 70
    format of, 22
    Gena character in, 31
    genre blending in, xv
    librarians and, xvi
    matching books to films, 58
    music pairing with, 82
    on *New York Times* Best Sellers list, 90
    old/new street lit, combining, 79
    publication of, 2
    reader completion of entire novel, 19
    romance in, 53
    as street-lit classic, 68, 69
trust, 39, 94
Turner, Dawn, 74
Turner, Nikki
    current-day fictional works by women, 9
    as established street-lit author, 72
    Girls from da Hood, 70
    A Hustler's Wife, 68, 69, 70
    A Project Chick, 57
    setting of stories by, 52
tweens
    Christian teen-friendly series, 46–47
    readers' advisory for, 43–47
    salient teen-friendly series, 44–46
    street lit for, 43–47
    toned-down street lit for, 42
twentieth-century classics, 109–110

twenty-first-century classics, 110–111

Tyree, Omar
   Flyy Girl, 68, 69
   old/new street lit, 79

U

Under Pressure (Hughes), 48–49
Upstate (Buckhanon), 22
urban, definition of, 27–28
Urban Books, x, 20, 72
urban erotica, 36–37
urban fiction
   classifying street lit as, 27–28
   description of, 12
   hip-hop, connection to, 105–106
   as LOC subject heading, 51
   street-lit genre classification, 11
   subgenres of, 28–29
   urban erotica *vs.*, 36–37
urban fiction cart, 59
Urban Reviews Online, 73

V

van Diepen, Allison, 47
Van Fleet, Connie, 39–40
Venkatesh, Sudhir, 55, 74
Verden, Claire E., 40
voice
   of author, 94
   author-reader connection and, 95
   of "the street," 13
   "the street" as silent antagonist, 14
   street lit empowers authors'/ readers' voices, 106
Volponi, Paul, 47

W

Wahida Clark Publishing, 8, 48–49
Walker, Alice, 13
War of the Bloods in My Veins: A Street Soldier's March toward Redemption (Morris), 74

Warner, Judith, 29
We Are All in the Dumps with Jack and Guy (Sendak), 23
We Beat the Street: How a Friendship Pact Led to Success (Davis, Jenkins, Hunt & Draper), 55
Weber, Carl
   The Family Business, 57, 68
   Kingpins series, 70
   street-fiction collections, established writers, 72
   Urban Books, x
"What's Hot!" collection, 78
Where There's Smoke (Little), 17, 32
White, Charmaine, 49
White, Joy, 55
White Lines: A Novel (Brown), 15
whites, 30
Whoreson (Goines), 5
Whyte, Anthony, 72
Wifebeater (Frisby), 33
Wifey (Swinson)
   in readers' advisory display, 57
   as street-lit classic, 68
   teen reading of, 42, 97
Wilke, Tachelle Shamash, 48
Williams, Brittani, 58
Williams, Dwan, 26
Williams, KaShamba
   Grimey, 25–26
   librarians and street lit, xvi
   old/new street lit, combining, 79
   teen-friendly street lit by, 23, 42, 43–44
Williams, Saul, 75
Williams, Stanley Tookie, 56
Williams, Terry, 74
Wilson, William Julius, 9
Wise, Alana, 24
A Wish after Midnight (Elliott)
   as speculative fiction, 18, 53
   as teen-friendly title, 48
women
   current-day fictional works by, 9

153

Index

women (*cont'd*)
    women's stories in street-lit
      genre, 30, 31
Woods, Teri
    author visits/events, 88
    book covers of, 24
    current-day fictional works by
      women, 9
    Dutch as street-lit classic, 68
    Dutch II: Angel's Revenge, 33
    Dutch trilogy, 8, 15, 58
    Dutch trilogy, Dutch character
      in, 31–32
    impact of books by, 69
    matching books to films for
      readers' advisory display, 58
    Meow Meow Productions, x
    in mystery genre, 53
    novels for addiction
      rehabilitation clients, 40
    old/new street lit, combining, 79
    setting of stories by, 52
    street-fiction collections,
      established writers, 72
    street-lit fiction series, 70
    teen book club and, 90
    True to the Game, xv, xvi, 2, 19
    True to the Game, as street-lit
      classic, 68
    True to the Game, format of, 22
    True to the Game, Gena
      character in, 31
    True to the Game, music pairing
      with, 82
    True to the Game, sales of, 6
Woodson, Jacqueline, 23
word associations, 87
Worth, Robert R., 4
Wright, Richard *Native Son*, 3–4,
    10, 54

nonfiction/fiction along
    historical continuum, 75
  novels by, xiv–xv
writing, 84
Wyatt, Neal, vii–viii

Y

Yasmin Peace series (Perry-Moore),
  46
Yates, Shanique, xi
The Year We Learned to Fly
  (Woodson), 23
Yekl: A Tale of the New York Ghetto
  (Cahan), 3
You Got Me Twisted (Dotson-Lewis),
  49
Young, Mallory, 28
young adult series, 115–116
young adult urban fiction
    recommended young adult
      titles, 48–49
    titles for foundational street-lit
      collection, 114–115
young adult (YA) literature
    street lit for tweens, 43–47
    street-lit titles for young adults,
      23–24
    teen-friendly titles, 48–49
    young adult series, 115–116
    young adult urban fiction,
      114–115

Z

Zanal Abidin, Nur Syazwanie, 40
Zane, xvi
Zangwill, Israel, 3
Zernike, Kate, 28
Zimmer, Melanie, 17

You may also be interested in...

ISBN: 978-0-8389-3861-4

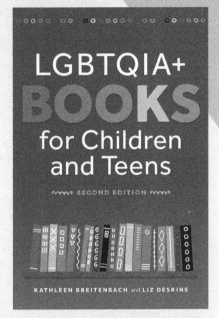

ISBN: 978-0-8389-3857-7

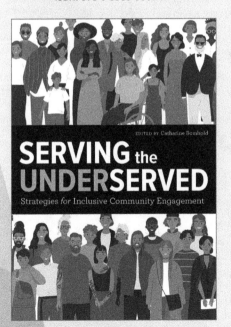

ISBN: 978-0-8389-3652-8

ISBN: 978-1-78330-597-1

For more titles, visit **alastore.ala.org**